Sexual Harassment and Schools of Social Work:
Issues, Costs, and Strategic Responses

Edited by

Marie Weil,
Michelle Hughes,
and
Nancy Hooyman

Council on Social Work Education
Alexandria, Virginia

Library of Congress Cataloging-in-Publication Data

Sexual harassment and schools of social work: issues, costs, and
    strategic responses / [edited] by Marie Weil, Michelle Hughes,
    and Nancy Hooyman
        p.   cm.
    Includes bibliographical references.
    ISBN 0-87293-040-8
    1. Social work education—United States.   2. Schools of social
work—United States.   3. Sexual harassment in colleges and
universities—United States.   4. Sexual harassment of women—
United States.   I. Weil, Marie Overby.   II. Hughes, Michelle, 1967- .
III. Hooyman, Nancy R.
HV11.S475   1994
361.3' 071' 073—dc20   94-19048
                                                                  CIP

Manufactured in the United States of America.

Table of Contents

Acknowledgment and Dedication   v

Foreword   vi
> Helen V. Graber, Chairperson
>> CSWE Commission on the Role and Status of Women

Introduction   1
Sexual Harassment and Schools of Social Work
> Marie O. Weil, Nancy R. Hooyman,
>> Terry L. Singer, and Helen V. Graber

Chapter 1   12
Sexual Harassment: Definitions,
> Policy Frameworks, and Legal Issues
>> Barbara W. Shank

Chapter 2   25
Sexual Harassment in Graduate Schools
> of Social Work: Provocative Dilemmas
>> Terry L. Singer

Chapter 3   39
Sexual Harassment in Social Work Field Placements
> Deborah Valentine, John Gandy,
>> Caroline Burry, and Leon Ginsberg

Chapter 4   54
Human and Institutional Costs of Sexual Harassment
> Terry L. Singer

Chapter 5   62
The Role of Male Administrators in Preventing
> and Responding to Sexual Harassment
>> Michael Reisch

Chapter 6   70
Planning for Prevention of Sexual Harassment
> at the University of Washington's School of Social Work
>> Nancy R. Hooyman and Lorraine Gutiérrez

Chapter 7   81
Sexual Harassment: Creating a Positive
    Environment for Learning
        Marie O. Weil, Nancy R. Hooyman, and Michelle Hughes

Selected Bibliography   95
        Beverly Koerin and Marie O. Weil

Appendix A   113
University Policies and Informational Materials
        San Francisco State University
        College of St. Catherine/University of St. Thomas
        University of Washington
        University of North Carolina, Chapel Hill

Appendix B   135
A Model Policy for Field Settings
        University of South Carolina

Appendix C   140
Educational and Training Materials
        College of St. Catherine/University of St. Thomas
        University of Washington

Acknowledgment and Dedication

Barbara Shank, Terry Singer, Nancy Hooyman, Michael Reisch, and Marie Weil have presented invitational sessions on sexual harassment in schools of social work at several Annual Program Meetings of CSWE. This collaboration has helped each of us learn more about how to handle this serious issue with regard to policy development and prevention.

In this publication, we are pleased to add the work of a team from the University of South Carolina's School of Social Work—Deborah Valentine, John Gandy, Caroline Burry, and Leon Ginsberg—who have focused on the issue of sexual harassment in field placements and provided a model field placement policy.

We would like to acknowledge the support of Helen Graber and the members of the CSWE Commission on the Role and Status of Women, who have encouraged our collaboration and the publication of this monograph. We particularly appreciate the contributions that commission members Beverly Koerin and Lorraine Gutiérrez have made to this project.

We dedicate this work to the social work students, known and unknown, who have had to struggle with sexual harassment and to the faculty who have helped them.

We hope this work will make a difference.

Foreword

The Council on Social Work Education's Commission on the Role and Status of Women has been working on heightening awareness among social work educators about sexual harassment for many years. Those of us involved have forgotten exactly how many presentations the Commission has sponsored at Annual Program Meetings. We have not, however, forgotten that the audiences started small and grew consistently larger, culminating in a well-attended invitational session at the 1992 APM. The presenters at that session, with other colleagues, are the authors of this monograph.

Why did those audiences start out so small? Was it because most of our colleagues didn't believe that sexual harassment was a problem in our schools and agencies? Now we know better, and it is largely because some social work educators used a tried-and-true social work principle: they asked those involved, namely administrators and students, about their experience with sexual harassment. It seems a long time ago that Terry Singer's groundbreaking piece, "Sexual Harassment in Graduate Schools of Social Work: Provocative Dilemmas" was published, but it was only in 1989.

Singer's presentation on sexual harassment at the 1988 APM sparked much professional discussion, some of it in the form of expressions of disbelief and skepticism: "These kinds of things don't happen in schools of social work!" Similar comments were heard in response to the specific sexual harassment case he described (with caution to conceal the identities of those involved): "The students must have had a vendetta against that teacher," "They were hysterical about poor grades," or "They were hysterical about being rejected by him." Much sympathy was expressed for the poor teacher and, in many discussions, he was perceived as the victim: "His reputation will be ruined," "He'll never work again," or "What about his family?" While it is important to recognize the losses that can be suffered by someone who engages in sexual harassment, it is crucial to recognize the harm done to the victims and to entire schools and departments.

We have made some progress away from the one-sided sympathetic response for the teacher. Following a number of serious sexual harassment incidents at several schools and departments, social work educators and administrators have begun to acknowledge that sexual harassment is a problem in our schools and field work agencies. This monograph is one effort by the Women's Commission and CSWE to assist departments and schools in dealing with sexual harassment through clear policies and procedures, fair processes, and most important, stronger preventive measures.

Sexual harassment is a complicated issue for administrators, teachers, and field instructors. For the students who are its victims, however, it can be life threatening. I know this to be true from my experience within two schools of social work, where it was my responsibility to deal with incidents of sexual harassment. The following "snapshots" of two female students illustrates the trauma for the victims of sexual harassment.

The first student I remember curled up in a chair in my office, as close to the fetal position as the chair and her body will allow, sobbing fitfully. She is bright and hard working, a person who has achieved much against great odds because of her determination to succeed. She has been so traumatized in the classroom, however, that she is willing to risk all that by being in my office. She is frightened and feels alone, even though she has confided in her roommate, who has been supportive and has finally convinced her to see me. She says she knows that it is the teacher who is at fault, but she sees no possible solution to her situation and even talks of suicide.

The second student I see sitting across the table from me with a file folder, some papers, and a notebook in which she intends to write down everything I say. I find out later that the notebook is a subterfuge; she actually is using a hidden tape recorder. She feels she has been forced to see me because of a complicated chain of events involving a teacher, an advisor, and a staff person. She seems frightened and hostile. She asserts that she wants to make no complaint against her field instructor, convinced that just being in my office will result in the teacher hearing that she complained and that she will suffer some related retribution. She knows that I can take no public action without her permission, and she wants taped proof that she has not given it. Eventually, when she discovers that my first priority is to protect her, she tells her story of continual physical and emotional sexual harassment.

These two young women were both graduate students in schools of social work. One white, one African American. Neither wanted to make a formal complaint. One of the most striking characteristics of each of these women was deep fear. Much recent discussion has centered on why women do not come forward; witnessing such fear made it easy for me to understand. The solutions are not so easy. Legal, educational, and personal issues complicate the problem for students, agencies, and schools. I hope that these snapshots have illustrated the importance of struggling to find solutions to the problem.

The Women's Commission of CSWE is pleased to present this monograph. It is a culmination of years of work on the problem of sexual harassment in schools of social work, and it is designed to assist faculty, administrators, field instructors, and students in understanding issues of sexual harassment, implementing positive policies and procedures, creating more positive educational climates, and developing preventive strategies to deal with this serious problem.

Helen Graber
Chairperson
CSWE Commission on the Role and Status of Women

Introduction:
Sexual Harassment
and Schools of Social Work

by Marie O. Weil, Nancy R. Hooyman, Terry L. Singer, and Helen V. Graber

S exual harassment is a critical issue that must be dealt with by schools and departments of social work in ways that are congruent with professional and academic values, supportive of equal treatment of those who have experienced harassment, and nondiscriminatory in relation to gender. At the federal level, sexual harassment is a violation of Title VII of the Civil Rights Act of 1964 and/or a violation of Title IX of the Education Amendments of 1972. It can occur either in *quid pro quo* demands for sexual favors or in the creation of an abusive or hostile environment. In the most recent case decided by the United States Supreme Court, *Harris v. Forklift Systems, Inc.* (November 9, 1993), the court unanimously confirmed its earlier opinions regarding hostile environments and further held that a violation of Title VII does not require that the persons harassed suffer injury or experience serious negative affects on their psychological well-being (*Harris v. Forklift Systems*, 1993). This decision strengthens legal protection against sexual harassment in the workplace and reinforces the notion of employers' responsibility in creating the work environment.

Social work administrators, educators, and practitioners should understand harassment as a legal and social issue and be prepared to deal with it in both educational and work environments. As a profession, social work is committed to the elimination of sexism. The Council on Social Work Education has taken a strong stance in

Marie Weil is Professor of Social Work at the University of North Carolina. Nancy Hooyman is Dean and Professor of Social Work at the University of Washington. Terry Singer is Dean of the School of Social Work at Marywood College. Helen Graber is Adjunct Professor at Webster University.

its Curriculum Policy Statement and Accreditation Standards against sexism, and harassment is one of its most virulent forms. This monograph provides information for schools and departments on the complex issues concerning sexual harassment, on procedures and remedies, and on strategies to prevent its occurrence.

The Broader Academic Context

National attention to the problems of sexual harassment generated by the Anita Hill-Clarence Thomas confrontation, the Tailhook scandal, the controversy surrounding Senator Bob Packwood of Oregon, the *Harris v. Forklift Systems* decision, and other media coverage has focused primarily on the workplace, and there is no doubt that such attention is needed in all work settings, including social work agencies and programs. Institutions of higher education, however, also face a very high risk of harassment occurrences because of the age and status differentials between students, support staff, and faculty. Social work students may be even more vulnerable than other students to the possibility of harassment because of their involvement in the formal academic setting of the classroom and the field placement environment. In other words, social work students may be in "double jeopardy" in relation to the risk of experiencing sexual harassment.

Sexual Harassment: Definitions and Conceptualizations

Sexual harassment is an abuse of power. It occurs when individuals with authority and position use their power to control or influence others' behavior. Environments characterized by unequal power relationships between individuals, such as classrooms, educational research projects, and field placements, pose great risk for students, junior faculty, and others who wield less power within the context of traditional academic relationships. This is clear with female students who, particularly in undergraduate settings, are young and relatively inexperienced, and therefore vulnerable to the power relationships explicit and implicit in student-faculty interactions. It is important to note, however, that students' reliance upon faculty for academic and career support applies not only to young, female students, but also to males and older female students. Graduate students are very much at risk because of the importance of the teacher-student relationship in their academic experiences. They rely heavily upon faculty for mentoring, career guidance and recommendations, and assistance with articles, theses, and dissertations.

Students in professional schools are particularly vulnerable to harassment because they frequently identify closely with faculty, look up to them as role models, and work with them in a variety of class, research, and field projects.

Thus, while concerns for economic survival and career advancement characterize the workplace, concerns for personal survival and career goals characterize the academy. The latter involves an entire "life script" for students that can be unalterably changed by a single incident of sexual harassment. Students usually feel pressure in their relationships with faculty in regard to grades, recommendations, or their career choices and employment opportunities. University and college settings then are characterized by both concerns for the educational, professional, and ethical development of students and concerns for the economic and career growth of faculty and staff.

In higher educational settings, sexual harassment most frequently takes place through the actions or words of an older male faculty member toward a younger female student. It is very important to bear in mind, however, that "while most harassers are men, most men are not harassers" (Bravo & Cassedy, 1992). University statistics typically illustrate a pattern of a small number of harassers with a large number of victims over time. Sexual harassment also affects other individuals and other relationships. It can happen between female faculty and male students or between members of the same sex. It can also occur between faculty, between faculty and staff, and in the case of peer harassment, it can occur between students. All incidents of harassment, regardless of those involved, are unethical and unprofessional. This monograph, however, primarily focuses upon the faculty-student relationship because of its centrality to the educational enterprise and because of the power inequities inherent in both the classroom and practicum settings.

Sexual Harassment between Faculty and Students

Sexual harassment between a faculty member and a student, whether in the classroom or field placement, represents an abuse of power by the faculty member who has authority over the student. It sexualizes the educational relationship and diverts energy from the expected roles of students and teachers. It may also sexually charge the learning environment in ways that are often negative, not only for the specific student, but also for others. Most students who encounter sexual harassment find the experience intimidating, embarrassing, demeaning, and frustrating. Reactions may range from lowered self-esteem or self-blame, to depression or suicidal thoughts, to anger and remedial action.

In addition to causing personal injury, sexual harassment incidents or patterns of harassing behavior can negatively impact the interactional climate of classrooms, field agencies, or even the entire school or department. Research on sexual harassment in academic settings indicates that such incidents or patterns have a chilling effect on both individual learning and collective behavior, including the learning and interaction environment of a program. Students and faculty may take sides when an incident of sexual harassment occurs. Such a split in the school community creates tensions among students, among faculty members, and between the two groups. Students may grow distrustful of faculty and administrators if they feel their concerns are not being addressed, and likewise, faculty may resent the increased attention to their behavior. The school community may become divided and cease to provide a supportive and safe educational environment for its members.

Addressing Sexual Harassment

Systemic attention to the issue of sexual harassment in college and university settings is a relatively new response to a problem that has long plagued campuses. This response grows out of long efforts, often initiated by female faculty and students, to analyze the effects of harassment on individuals and the educational process. It has taken nearly a decade—a decade punctuated by scandals that have rocked departments and universities—to focus sufficient attention on sexual harassment as a serious, common, and disabling problem in higher education.

Although sexual harassment has gained recognition as a growing, contemporary phenomenon, varied opinions have emerged about how to approach it. These opinions are framed by personal experience and values, events in the media, and conceptualizations of power and gender inequities. It is incumbent upon social work educators to recognize the risks these issues pose to the academy, to analyze the problems, and to seek remedies. This monograph represents one such effort, addressing the realities of sexual harassment in the classroom and field educational enterprise. It has grown out of the work of the CSWE Women's Commission, which has sponsored several special sessions at Annual Program Meetings focusing on sexual harassment and its impact on social work students, faculties, and staffs. Responses to those sessions prompted recognition of the need for a more comprehensive way to address the issue in social work education, to provide more relevant information, and to develop policies and processes to deal with harassment issues.

The classroom provides the obvious and first forum for developing an understanding of the issues related to sexual harassment. In schools of social work, it is expected that forms of oppression will be systematically analyzed and understood. The Council on Social Work Education explicitly expects schools to demonstrate classroom content which is nonsexist and which prepares students to deal with sexism in practice, programs, and policies. The learning most internalized by students, however, may take place outside the classroom in the metamessages of those intrinsically bound to the academy. The academy, with its relationships among students, faculty, administrators, and practicum instructors, provides a veritable laboratory for modeling behavior that affirms human dignity and purpose. It is essential, therefore, that social work administrators, faculty, and field personnel develop proactive policies and act to eliminate sexism throughout the organization and its practicum sites, not just in the classroom. Such efforts can help create a supportive learning environment that is congruent with individual dignity, freedom, autonomy, and positive professional development. Given social work's commitment to equity and social justice, professional values and ethics should be modeled throughout the entire educational process.

Social work faculty have many important reasons for addressing issues of sexual harassment. First, we have a value base and professional Code of Ethics predicated on the fundamental worth of and respect for all persons. This value base should apply not only to interactions with clients but with students as well. Second, typically over 80% of social work students are women whose experiences, aspirations, and lives' work are being framed within our institutions. An incident of sexual harassment can cause serious and long-term harm to an individual's career and personal life. Third, we are educating people to become helping professionals who can bring out the best in others and positively transform organizations and social systems. Therefore, modeling of respectful and appropriate behavior assumes great importance. Fourth, social work's professional mission is incompatible with behavior that is harassing or demeaning to individuals because of gender, race, sexual orientation, or other individual characteristics. Finally, by and large social workers and social work educators seek to "do the right thing" just because it *is* the right thing. It is important that prevention and procedures dealing with sexual harassment become normal facets of social work education programs in their overall pursuit of excellence and professional development.

Sexual harassment is a complicated problem, and addressing it is a challenge. As this monograph makes clear, legal, psychological, social, professional, and educational issues surround it, and lives are at stake. As the first step in overcoming a problem is to understand it, then the following presentation of issues is the way to begin.

The Power Differential

Sexual harassment is not just a sexual issue. In many ways it is not even *primarily* a sexual issue. It raises significant problems of oppression, power, and control. The power differential is very clear in the classroom and in field settings; even when students and teachers attempt to equalize their respective roles, the institution gives the teacher grading and possibly recommendation and reference power over the student. Power, therefore, is an inevitable part of the teacher-student relationship. The same power differential applies to administrators, who may be advisers as well. Recognition of the power differential has caused some colleges and universities to prohibit any relationships (consensual or otherwise) between school or departmental personnel and students.

The power differential is also present in social work field practica. Students may be vulnerable to harassment from their field instructors, other agency staff, or even board members. Since students typically view their practicum as the place where they learn to be professionals, they may be even more vulnerable to problematic behavior in that setting. In addition, a field instructor's recommendation is often the most critical reference for future jobs, thus, students may fear reporting harassment by a field instructor—particularly if the person is well known and respected in the profession.

In sexual harassment policies, power is portrayed as emanating from position status grounded in faculty or administrative authority. There are, however, different kinds of power affecting gender relationships that may not be acknowledged in schools of social work. For example, the physical strength and social power of men have traditionally placed women in subordinate positions. Male students have used these basic power forms to intimidate and harass female classmates, as have male clients who harass student interns. Agencies should recognize these risks and prepare students to deal with them. In universities and colleges, student-to-student harassment is typically handled by the student judicial system. That venue is increasingly being challenged, however, and schools and departments of social work need to consider their responses to these abuses of power and their potential effect on the organizational climate.

Furthermore, race and ethnicity can be components of harassment; and in this case historical issues of power and discrimination can cause further complications. Differing patterns of communication can also create tensions between men and women, especially when they are of different ethnic or racial backgrounds. And finally, harassment between members of the same sex brings up a number of complex power issues that have yet to be fully addressed by the literature. In such instances, students may feel even more reluctant to report because of concerns for privacy, fears of homophobic reactions from other administrators, faculty, or students, and lack of institutional support.

Reporting and Students' Rights

When they are victimized by sexual harassment, students have the practical and legal right to determine for themselves how they want to proceed, or not proceed, with complaints about sexual harassment. Some victims, for purposes of confidentiality or other reasons, may wish to address the behavior themselves. Women's organizations, rape crisis centers, and other concerned advocates suggest that students send a letter to the harasser stating that the specified behavior is perceived as harassing and is unwelcome. This letter should note the date and location when the behavior occurred and should include as many details as possible. Students should then send the letter by registered mail to the harasser, keep a copy for themselves, and give a copy to at least one other person as documentation that the problem exists. Such documentation is sought by attorneys if the matter is ever adjudicated. Often, the letter itself is sufficient to stop the unwanted behavior with the particular student.

A second option for students is to report the harassment to a trusted faculty member, to the director, dean, or associate dean of the school or program, or to the university dean of students. Universities vary in their reporting procedures and may include other types of reporting mechanisms such as departmental or university ombudsmen. Such individuals can provide the support and guidance the student needs to resolve the problem, and if desired, will help the student file a complaint on a higher university level. Most universities and colleges have a hierarchy of reporting options that emphasize problem solving within the department or school as a first step. It is important that students know that they retain the right to report or not. A mechanism to provide a confidential consultation for the student is crucial; otherwise, students may remain silent.

Some institutions, however, are responding to their legal responsibility to follow up on charges of sexual harassment by eliminating this confidential consultation. Conflict can arise between the student's desire for confidentiality and the institution's need to address a serious and often repetitive situation. For example, an administrator may be aware that a student is the fourth or eighth person to report harassment by a particular faculty member; but if all students claim confidentiality and do not want to proceed to a formal report, the school or department is unable to address the serious problem. Another related problem can arise if students, for fear that confidentiality will not be honored, do not report incidents of harassment. In fact, they may confide in no one and continue to blame themselves for the incident.

Rights of the Accused

The rights of the accused must be protected. An allegation of harassment does not prove guilt, but even an allegation can cloud a reputation. Since allegations of sexual harassment can jeopardize a faculty member's career, schools and departments of social work must make every effort to establish procedures that are fair and that protect both parties. Accused faculty members may not perceive their behavior as intimidating or harassing, but they should clearly understand the program's policies regarding harassment, the need for confidentiality, and the process for adjudication.

Toll on the Victim and Others

Sexual harassment is known to take a heavy toll on the victim, but all parties involved, including those who must handle the complaint and the alleged harasser, are adversely affected. Victims often agonize over whether or not to report incidents or proceed with complaints. If they do proceed, victims may face a tension-filled adjudication process. But all members of the academic community experience an impact from either rumors or a formal procedure. Schools or departments risk being divided into warring camps that create a negative effect on the entire academic community.

Policies and Procedures to Deal with Sexual Harassment

Concern for the image of a school or department and its relationship with the university or college must be taken into account, but cannot be allowed to prevent policies and procedures from being developed and implemented. Information about sexual harassment, including its definitions and a description of the process to follow if harassment occurs, should be given to students upon entering a social work program. There is no evidence that such information exacerbates the problem or leads to false accusations.

As noted, social work administrators and faculty must consider how to create and sustain positive and safe learning environments for all members of their educational community. As a first step, schools and departments of social work must develop up-to-date, legally analyzed and approved policies and procedures for dealing with incidents of sexual harassment. Typically, sexual harassment is included in specific university or college policies, but schools or departments of social work will need additional policies to guide the protection of students in field placements. Issues of harassment among students are generally handled through student courts or administrative procedures, while those among faculty members are handled through school, departmental, and institutional-level inquiry and review.

Because of the power differential between faculty/administrators and students, and the interaction between sexuality and power, sexual harassment is a potential problem in all schools and departments. In addition to policies and procedures, practice strategies and a clear problem-solving and adjudication process are needed.

Prevention

While most schools have developed policies for dealing with sexual harassment, far too few have adopted preventive approaches. Establishing a climate of safety and security for all students, clarifying role boundaries between students and faculty, and educating students about the potential for harassment can build an organizational culture that discourages harassment. Potential exists to prevent sexual harassment through clear statements prohibiting certain behaviors and through workshops, seminars, and other programs to sensitize faculty, students, and agency field instructors to the issues involved.

In terms of prevention, social workers can bring special skill to issues of sexual harassment. For more than two decades social work practitioners and academics have provided leadership in the difficult practice areas of sexual abuse and abuse prevention. For at least a decade academics have incorporated information on sexual abuse of young children into the curriculum. Both academics and practitioners emphasize children's intuitive recognition of "bad touch" and unwanted physical intimacy. Children are now regularly taught that if they get the "uh-oh" feeling, something is wrong in the situation. They need to say no, yell, or attempt to get away. Children are also taught that if abuse occurs, it is not their fault; adults are responsible for their own behavior.

This same sense of uneasiness—the "uh-oh" feeling—is experienced by many victims of sexual harassment. In a typical situation the victim feels infringed upon or trapped. As sociologist Susan Marshall has stated: "Men don't understand that caged feeling. But women know what sexual harassment is. It's when your neck hairs stand up and you feel like you're being stalked" (as cited in Kantrowitz, 1992, p. 16). If social workers can effectively work with young children to prepare them for the risks of danger and exploitation, surely social work educators can do the same for their students. Students need to receive accurate information about the reality of harassment in the academic community and in the workplace. They need to be encouraged to trust their perceptions and to act to protect themselves, other students, and clients.

Organization of Monograph

This volume describes educational and planning initiatives for responding to and preventing harassment. It is dedicated to providing information that social work programs can use to improve learning environments and to develop proactive and supportive policies, procedures, and plans for dealing with this serious social, educational, and professional problem.

The first chapter provides the legal definition of sexual harassment, describes legal issues that schools face, and delineates policy frameworks needed to deal with the issue. The second and third chapters discuss the knowledge base on sexual harassment in schools of social work. Chapter 2 presents results from a survey of schools of social work regarding incidents of sexual harassment and administrators' concerns. Chapter 3 discusses and analyzes data from a recent survey of schools of social work about sexual harassment in field settings; the authors emphasize the need for a specific policy covering field practica.

Chapter 4 presents the range and severity of human and institutional costs for schools and departments that must deal with harassment and its aftermath. Chapter 5 discusses the actions that male administrators can take to prevent and respond to sexual harassment. The sixth chapter describes a schoolwide plan to develop and implement prevention strategies for dealing with sexual and other forms of harassment, and also discusses implications for social work education. The concluding chapter discusses reactions to the complex issues surrounding sexual harassment and how schools of social work can address those reations to create a positive learning environment. Also provided as part of the volume is an extensive bibliography on the topic and three appendices that provide samples of general sexual harassment policies, a specialized field practicum policy, and training materials useful in educating students, faculty, and staff about sexual harassment, its prevention, and its remedies. All of these materials may be used to develop sexual harassment information sessions and prevention strategies that fit the needs of particular schools and departments.

The authors acknowledge that it is a complex task to build an excellent social work program—to develop an educational environment in which ideas are openly discussed and analyzed and in which students are prepared for effective practice. Institutional barriers, established professional values, school philosophies and interests, and instructor and student biases all influence the educational environment. If this already complex environment is impacted by abuse of power in any form, including sexual harassment, seemingly impossible barriers to learning are established.

In the interest of creating safe and healthy environments in which to learn and work, this volume challenges the reader to explore organizational and professional boundaries, to promote systems that are free of gender bias and concomitant harassment, and to reaffirm the values of the profession in terms of human dignity. The price for ignoring sexual harassment as a larger social issue and as a special concern for the academic environment is too great for society and for the profession to bear.

References

Bravo, E., & Cassedy, E. (1992). *The 9 to 5 guide to combating sexual harassment. Candid advice from 9 to 5—the National Association of Working Women*. New York: John Wiley & Sons.

Harris v. Forklift Systems, Inc. 114 S. Ct. 367 (1993).

Kantrowitz, B. (1992). Sexual harassment in America: An overview. In C. Wekesser, K.L. Swisher, & C. Pierce (Eds.), *Sexual harassment* (pp. 16-24). San Diego: Greenhaven Press.

1

Sexual Harassment: Definitions, Policy Frameworks, and Legal Issues

by Barbara W. Shank

S exual harassment is an old problem but a new issue. Since the Clarence Thomas/Anita Hill hearings, sexual harassment has been the subject of increased attention in the media, the workplace, and the classroom. As a result, society is finally willing to acknowledge the existence of this problem, and victims are increasingly willing to confront the problem directly. Both women and men are engaging in discussion—sometimes friendly, sometimes combative— on the myriad complex issues surrounding sexual harassment. They are analyzing and challenging traditional patterns of behavior. They are tracing relationships between sexual harassment and other types of oppressive behavior, such as racism and homophobia. And consequently, they are gaining knowledge and awareness about the existence and pervasiveness of sexual harassment, and about the laws that prohibit such discriminatory behavior. Such knowledge is vital in the effort to eradicate sexual harassment from our workplaces, schools, and personal relationships. It is also vital for those interested in protecting themselves, their employees, and their students from the damages caused by harassing behavior.

Schools of social work have not been exempt from incidents of sexual harassment or from the controversy regarding the subtle issues that surround the problem. Many schools are taking steps to prevent sexual harassment and to respond more effectively and sensitively to allegations. In their efforts to address these issues, departments and schools of social work need information regarding

Barbara Shank is Chair of the Department of Social Work, College of St. Catherine/ University of St. Thomas.

Material in this article concerning the November 1993 Supreme Court case *Harris v. Forklift Systems, Inc.* was contributed by Marie Weil, Professor of Social Work at the University of North Carolina, Chapel Hill.

policy guidelines, legal issues, and types of sexual harassment. This chapter will discuss the legal constructs and implications of sexual harassment, the types and elements of sexually harassing behavior, and issues specific to sexual harassment in academic settings.

General Background

Sexual harassment is pervasive in our society; it is also illegal. It is clearly an abuse of power and a violation of professional ethics. It creates a discriminatory climate and disrupts both the workplace routine and the educational process. Despite the emotional and economic costs for those associated with sexual harassment, it occurs in all types of organizations, institutions, and occupations. Scholars have documented its existence from the time "women began trading their labor in the marketplace" (Bularzik, 1978), and recent studies demonstrate that a large number of women experience sexual harassment within all segments of our society (Adams, Kottke, & Padgitt, 1983; Bailey & Richards, 1985; Gutek, 1985; Shank & Johnston, 1986).

Consistently, research on sexual harassment has indicated that nearly all harassers are male. Because women generally hold less organizational power than men, they are more vulnerable to unwelcome sexual advances and other forms of harassment. One must remember that the primary motive in sexual harassment is not sexual desire, but power. In addition, although 95% of harassers are male, men as well as women can be victims of sexual harassment, women can be harassers, and harassment can occur between members of the same sex.

In the mid-1970s, as the general public became aware of sexual harassment, this country made initial progress in addressing the problem. For the first time, victims began to discuss their experiences openly and organizations began to develop measures to deal with sexual harassment incidents (Karsten & Kramer, 1985). In 1977, four court decisions established precedents for the illegality of sexual harassment in the workplace under Title VII of the 1964 Civil Rights Act: *Barnes v. Costle*; *Tomkins v. Public Service Electric & Gas Co.*; *Garber v. Saxon Business Products*; and *Heelan v. Johns-Manville Corp.* (Center for Women Policy Studies, 1981). New federal legislation, issued by the Equal Employment Opportunity Commission (EEOC) in 1980, provided guidelines that specifically defined sexual harassment in employment settings (Center for Women Policy Studies, 1981). Since then, many employers have adopted policies and internal guidelines for dealing with complaints of sexual harassment. The effectiveness of these policies, however, varies across settings in terms of policy development and implementation.

While most of the literature discusses sexual harassment in the corporate sector, sexual harassment also occurs in academic settings. The problem of sexual harassment in higher education became nationally recognized in 1977 with *Alexander v. Yale University*. In this case, Yale University was sued by a student for having an inadequate policy for handling charges of sexual harassment. This suit, along with the 1980 EEOC guidelines, was the impetus for the formulation of sexual harassment policies by several institutions of higher education. It also spurred similar reports from other universities, indicating that incidents such as those at Yale were not isolated cases (Maihoff and Forrest, 1983).

Currently, nearly all colleges and universities, at least in policy, strongly condemn any behavior which constitutes sexual harassment. This behavior includes actions by supervisors toward their staff and actions between faculty and students. Some schools of social work have also developed their own sexual harassment policies to cover actions by fieldwork instructors and students.

An individual who has been the victim of sexual harassment in an academic setting has many options. The victim may resolve the harassment through an informal process, initiate a complaint through the college or university's formal sexual harassment policy guidelines, or file a civil or criminal suit. Laws exist to protect individuals from sexual harassment; the key is to understand what rights these laws protect and how they define sexual harassment.

Statutory Bases and Definitions of Sexual Harassment

In most areas of the country, there are four statutory bases for sexual harassment: Title VII of the Civil Rights Act of 1964, Title IX of the Education Amendments of 1972, state-enacted human rights acts, and city ordinances.

Title VII of the 1964 Civil Rights Act

Title VII of the 1964 Civil Rights Act, which prohibits sex discrimination in the workplace, has provided the primary statutory basis for sexual harassment cases. Section 703(a) of Title VII provides: "It shall be unlawful employment practice for an employer to discriminate against any individual with respect to [her or] his compensation, terms, conditions, or privileges of employment because of such individual's race, color, religion, sex, or national origin." Since the late 1970s, the courts have broadly interpreted Title VII and have found that workplace sexual harassment is clearly prohibited as a form of sexual discrimination.

Title VII has also been used as the basis for other federal legislation regarding sexual harassment. In 1980, the EEOC established a definition of sexual harassment and developed a framework for reviewing sexual harassment claims. The EEOC "established criteria for determining when unwelcome conduct of a sexual nature constitutes sexual harassment, defined the circumstances under which an employer may be held liable, and suggested affirmative steps an employer should take to prevent sexual harassment" (Conte, 1990, p. 481). This set of guidelines further extends the definition of actionable sexual harassment as established by the previous court decisions (Center for Women Policy Studies, 1981). The guidelines, issued on November 10, 1980, define sexual harassment as follows:

> Unwelcome sexual advances, requests for sexual favors, and other verbal or physical conduct of a sexual nature constitute sexual harassment when:
> (1) submission to such conduct is made either explicitly or implicitly a term or condition of an individual's employment;
> (2) submission to or rejection of such conduct by an individual is used as the basis for employment decisions affecting such individual; or
> (3) such conduct has the purpose or effect of unreasonably interfering with an individual's work performance or creating an intimidating, hostile, or offensive work environment. (Equal Employment Opportunity Commission, 1980)

The EEOC guidelines are aimed at sexual harassment that causes "concrete economic detriment to the victim" or results in "creating an unproductive or an offensive working environment" (Conte, 1990, p. 27). The guidelines broadened the definition of actionable sexual harassment by acknowledging that sexually harassing behavior which creates a hostile work environment is a violation of Title VII.

In 1986, the Supreme Court adopted the EEOC definition of sexual harassment in *Meritor Savings Bank v. Vinson*. In this case, the Court recognized that sexual harassment claims are not limited to those for which a tangible job benefit is withheld, stating that a plaintiff may prove discrimination based on sex when harassment has created an offensive, discriminatory work environment. This Supreme Court decision "held 'without question' that sexual harassment is a form of sex discrimination and that hostile environment as well as *quid pro quo* harassment violates Title VII. This decision was significant as it legitimized this area of the law for complainants and put employers and harassers on notice that unwelcome sexual conduct will not be tolerated in the workplace" (Conte, 1990, p. 52).

In November 1993, in *Harris v. Forklift Systems, Inc.*, the Supreme Court upheld the *Meritor* standard and further clarified issues related to findings of a discriminatorily "abusive" or "hostile" work environment. The Court found that sexual harassment under Title VII does not demand a level of proof documenting injury or serious effect on psychological well-being. As Justice O'Connor states in the Supreme Court's unanimous opinion:

> Title VII comes into play before the harassing conduct leads to a nervous breakdown. . . . Certainly Title VII bars conduct that would seriously affect a reasonable person's psychological well-being, but the statute is not limited to such conduct. So long as the environment would reasonably be perceived and is perceived as hostile or abusive . . . there is no need for it also to be psychologically injurious. (*Harris v. Forklift Systems, Inc.*, 1993, pp. 370-371)

But how does one objectively determine when a work environment "would reasonably be perceived" as hostile or abusive? Justice O'Connor states:

> We can say that whether an environment is "hostile" or "abusive" can be determined only by looking at all the circumstances. These may include the frequency of the discriminatory conduct; its severity; whether it is physically threatening or humiliating, or a mere offensive utterance; and whether it unreasonably interferes with an employee's psychological well-being is, of course relevant to determining whether the plaintiff actually found the environment abusive. But while psychological harm, like any other relevant factor, may be taken into account, no single factor is required. (*Harris v. Forklift Systems, Inc.*, 1993, p. 371)

Thus, while psychological harm may be taken into account when reviewing the circumstances, it is not *required* to prove that sexual harassment occurred. The precedent set in *Harris* carries great significance for the workplace, and its principles may well be used in subsequent cases.

Title IX of the 1972 Education Amendments

Title VII clearly addresses sex discrimination in employment, but it does not cover students who are sexually harassed by faculty members, because students are not employees of the university. Faculty/student sexual harassment is covered under Title IX of the Education Amendments of 1972, which provides: "No person in the U.S. shall, on the basis of sex, be excluded from participation in, be denied the benefits of, or be subjected to discrimination under any education program or activity receiving federal financial assistance" (20 U.S.C.1681a). Title IX covers both employment and educational settings. Like Title VII of the Civil Rights Act, Title IX prohibits discrimination on the basis of sex. As sexual harassment is a form of discrimination, it constitutes a violation of Title IX.

Title IX requires colleges and universities to establish adequate grievance procedures for alleged violations and to guarantee prompt investigation of complaints and proper remedial measures. Failure to do so may result in loss of federal funding. The key to Title IX enforcement has been this threatened loss of federal financial assistance—which has been interpreted to include student financial aid.

State Human Rights Acts and City Ordinances

Through human rights legislation, states have begun to address the issue of sexual harassment. Most states have enacted antidiscrimination legislation and 49 states have specifically addressed sexual harassment as a form of sex discrimination. In each state where sexual harassment has been addressed by act, the state legislature has established a specific definition of sexual harassment. In addition, at the local level, many cities have developed specific ordinances that address sexual harassment both in employment and in education. The establishment of state acts and local ordinances contributes to the goal of eliminating employment and educational discrimination and provides additional avenues for victims of sexual harassment to seek appropriate resolution of their complaints.

Types of Sexual Harassment

The EEOC guidelines define two types of sexual harassment: *quid pro quo* harassment and environmental harassment. A third type, defined as sexual favoritism, has emerged more recently in the literature.

Quid pro quo sexual harassment occurs when "submission to or rejection of such [sexual] conduct by an individual is used as the basis for employment or educational decisions affecting the individual" (Conte, 1990, p. 482). Situations in which *quid pro quo* harassment has been found include: requests by a supervisor or faculty member for after-hours social activities; repeated sexual remarks or repeated suggestions that engaging in a sexual affair would enhance employment or educational opportunities; and sexual advances which, when resisted, led to an adverse employment or educational decision impacting the employee or student (e.g., transfer, poor evaluation, lay-off, dismissal, or poor grade) (Cole, 1992).

In situations involving *quid pro quo* sexual harassment, victims must establish that:

- they belong to a protected group,
- they were subject to unwelcome sexual advances,
- the conduct complained of was in fact based upon sex,
- the conduct complained of affected the victim's employment or educational benefits,
- negative consequences resulted when the victim failed to comply with advances or demands, and
- the employer knew or should have known about the harassment (Conte, 1990).

In *quid pro quo* actions, employers are held liable for the sexual harassment of an employee or student if the harassment is committed by anyone under the control of the agency or institution (Conte, 1990).

Environmental sexual harassment, the second type, involves sexual harassment that creates a hostile or abusive work or educational environment. Victims of hostile environmental harassment do not have to prove that a tangible job or educational benefit was withheld or that the harassment caused other detrimental economic consequences. They must, however, demonstrate that the harassment was sufficiently severe or pervasive to unreasonably interfere with an individual's performance or to create an "intimidating, hostile, or offensive environment" (Conte, 1990, p. 56). Victims must also show that the discrimination was based on sex, that the conduct was not just an isolated incident, and that the employer knew or should have known of the hostile environment and failed to take prompt remedial action (Aaron, 1993; Conte, 1990).

A third type of sexual harassment that has recently emerged in the literature is termed "sexual favoritism" or "reverse *quid pro quo*."

This type of harassment involves gender-based sexual favoritism that has an adverse effect on the employment or educational opportunities of *other* employees. An employee who is passed over for employment opportunities or benefits because another employee submitted to an employer's or supervisor's request for sexual favors may have a cause for action under Title VII. However, if both men and women were disadvantaged for reasons other than gender, then sexual favoritism may be deemed unfair, but it does not constitute discrimination on the basis of sex (Conte, 1990; Karasov, 1990).

Elements of Sexual Harassment

A review of the literature identifies several critical elements of sexual harassment which include power, gender, sex, and "unwelcomeness." The bottom line of all sexual harassment is power. "When a formal power differential exists, all sexist or sexual behavior is seen as harassment, since the woman is not considered to be in a position to object, resist or give fully free consent" (Fitzgerald, 1990, p. 24). To be defined as sexual harassment, conduct must consist of verbal or physical activity of a sexual nature, imposed on the basis of sex. Victims must establish that, but for the fact of their sex, they would not have been the target of the harassment. Another critical element in defining sexual harassment involves unwelcomeness. Sexual advances must be unwelcome to be unlawful. Courts have established that to prove unwelcomeness, the victim must show that the conduct was undesirable or offensive and that it was unsolicited and unwanted (Conte, 1990).

Verbal or Physical Conduct

The specific verbal, nonverbal, or physical conduct that may constitute sexually harassing behavior is often determined on a case-by-case basis. Verbal behaviors that may constitute sexual harassment include "sexual slurs, sexual propositions, pressure for sexual activity, comments about a woman's body, asking intimate or embarrassing questions, making harassing telephone calls, boasting of sexual conquests, sexist comments, threats and homophobic remarks" (Conte, 1990, p. 80). Nonverbal behavior that may constitute sexual harassment includes looking up women's skirts or down their blouses; taking unwelcome photographs; making suggestive or insulting sounds, whistles, or obscene gestures; ogling; and dropping trousers or engaging in other forms of indecent exposure (Conte,

1990). Physical conduct that may constitute sexual harassment ranges from touching, patting, pinching, or massaging, to fondling, kissing, or raping (Conte, 1990). In addition to these behaviors, the physical environment can be found to be offensive when sexually explicit cartoons, calendars, literature, photographs, or sexual graffiti are displayed, or when revealing uniforms are required (Conte, 1990).

Another view of sexually harassing behaviors has been presented by Fitzgerald, who views sexual harassment along a continuum. She places gender harassment on one end; seductive behavior, sexual bribery, and sexual coercion in the middle; and sexual assault on the other end (Fitzgerald et al., 1988). This view expands the definition of sexual harassment by illustrating the full range of behaviors covered by legal definitions and experienced by women.

Sexual Harassment in Academe

There is a growing awareness on campuses that sexual harassment is a major problem that disrupts the educational process. Students who experience sexual harassment often suffer adverse emotional, psychological, economic, and physical reactions. For example, students often change their educational programs, their performance in course work suffers, and many drop out of school (Paludi, 1990).

Dziech and Weiner (1984) reported that nearly 30% of undergraduate women are victims of sexual harassment during their four years in college, although only 2–3% are likely to report the incident (Robertson, Dyer, & Campbell, 1985). Adams et al. (1983) reported that when gender harassment (generalized sexist statements and behavior that convey insulting, degrading, and/or sexist attitudes) is added to the definition of sexual harassment, the percentage of those who experience sexual harassment as undergraduate women increases to nearly 70%. Bailey and Richards (1985) reported that the incidence rate of sexual harassment for women graduate students and faculty is even higher than the rates for undergraduate women. Other surveys of sexual harassment on campus have found that between 10% and 33% of female students have reported being sexually harassed at their universities (Benson & Thomson, 1982; Metha & Nigg, 1983; Ross & Green, 1983; Shank & Johnston, 1986; Whitmore, 1983; Wilson & Kraus, 1983).

As with supervisor/staff harassment, sexual harassment of students is characterized by an imbalance of power. Students are made vulnerable to incidents of harassment because of their status within a department, as well as their dependency upon faculty for grades, recommendations, and career guidance. Due to fear of reprisal, they may neither report the incident formally or informally, nor tell other students, friends, or advisers. Despite these complicating factors, students are protected from sexual harassment under Title IX of the 1972 Education Amendments, which address *quid pro quo* sexual harassment. The courts as yet have not allowed hostile environment harassment claims to be filed under Title IX (Cole, 1992).

Consensual Relationships

The regulation of consensual relationships by colleges and universities is a hotly debated issue. These types of relationships present a problem for institutions of higher education because federal law does not ban them among employees. Those who oppose regulation of consensual relationships cite First Amendment rights, the right to freedom of association, and rights of academic freedom, which include faculty autonomy and self-regulation. Those who favor institutional regulation stress the inherent imbalance of power in supervisor/staff and faculty/student relationships that prohibits the formation of a truly consensual relationship. Colleges and universities have generally refrained from forbidding consensual relationships, but they have begun to warn supervisors and faculty members about the liability of entering into a relationship where the power differential is so great between the two parties. They stress the risk that the subordinates or students will feel compelled to enter into relationships with supervisors or faculty members through fear of retaliation or other adverse consequences. College and university policies usually state that the "subordinate's or student's consent to the intimate relationship is no defense to a subsequent claim of sexual harassment brought by the subordinate or student" (Karasov, 1990, p. 15).

Institutional Liability and Remedies for Sexual Harassment

Institutions may be held liable for sexual harassment by their employees if they knew or should have known of the harassing conduct and failed to provide prompt and equitable resolution of the complaint. Institutions can be held liable for both *quid pro quo* and hostile environment harassment. Employers at risk are those that fail to institute a policy against sexual harassment or establish a

mechanism for handling complaints that arise. Even when employers have sexual harassment policies and grievance procedures in
place, they may still be held liable if the procedures were not
effective to remedy the situation (Karasov, 1990; Conte, 1990).

Both Title VII and Title IX provide definite remedies for victims
of sexual harassment. Once the victim has proven that a violation
occurred and liability has been assigned, the courts may award
several types of restitution, including reinstatement and/or back pay,
payment of attorneys' fees, injunctions against further discrimination by the harasser, or "any equitable relief as the court deems
appropriate" (Conte, 1990, p. 212). In a violation of Title IX,
withdrawal of federal funds is the statutory remedy. However,
because this action is not considered an effective remedy for the
victim, other relief is also available. Recently, monetary damages
have been awarded to victims under Title IX (Conte, 1990), and state
and local statutes may also provide compensatory damages, reinstatement, back pay, payment of attorneys' fees, or punitive damages
(Karasov, 1990).

Affirmative Institutional Response

To protect their employees and themselves from liability, institutions of higher education must develop policies and procedures
that prohibit sexual harassment. Policies should prohibit *quid pro
quo* and hostile environment harassment in all employment/educa-
tional settings. Policies should also prohibit retaliation against any
individual making a complaint, and should define and include examples of harassing behavior. They should clearly state the complaint mechanism—outlining the channels through which harassment
should be reported, assigning responsibility for complaint investigation to specific individuals, and providing official guidelines for
complaint investigation. Procedures for investigating complaints
must be carefully followed to ensure fairness and uniformity of
investigations. Appendix A of this volume includes sample sexual
harassment policies from several universities.

Conclusion

The sexual harassment literature clearly shows that sexual harassment takes place in professional, social, religious, and educational environments. It is pervasive in the workplace and on college
and university campuses; a lack of complaints does not mean that

sexual harassment does not occur. It can happen to anyone, anywhere, regardless of position or personal characteristics.

Sexual harassment involves an abuse of power, and should not be confused with sexual desire. It can exist wherever men and women work together in unequal work relationships, interacting with each other in supervisor/supervisee or faculty/student roles. Social work students are vulnerable to sexual harassment in the classroom and in field placements as well.

As social work educators and practitioners, we must strive to better understand the dynamics of this problem and to prepare our students to deal with it effectively. Colleges and universities must adopt policies that prohibit sexual harassment and establish clear procedures for addressing complaints. Departments and schools of social work must do the same. If sexual harassment is not addressed, it may undermine an institution's ability to maintain a productive working and learning environment.

Sexual harassment will never be completely eliminated, but it can be reduced in frequency, intensity, and duration. The first step that must be taken is to establish academic and work environments that expose, discourage, and censure harassment of all kinds.

References

Aaron, T. E. (1993). *Sexual harassment in the workplace: A guide to the law and a research overview for employers and employees.* Jefferson, NC: McFarland & Co.

Adams, J. E., Kottke, J. L., & Padgitt, J. S. (1983). Sexual harassment of university students. *Journal of College Student Personnel, 24,* 484-490.

Alexander v. Yale University, 459 F. Supp. 1 (D. Conn. 1977), *aff'd,* 631 F 2nd 178 (2nd Cir. 1980).

Barnes v. Costle, 561 F. 2d 983 (3rd Cir. 1977).

Bailey, N., & Richards, M. (1985). *Tarnishing the ivory tower: Sexual harassment in graduate training programs.* Paper presented at the Annual Meeting of the American Psychological Association, Los Angeles.

Benson, D. J., & Thomson, G. E. (1982). Sexual harassment on a university campus: The confluence of authority relations, sexual interest and gender stratification. *Social Problems, 29,* 236-251.

Bularzik, M. (1978). Sexual harassment at the workplace: Historical notes. *Radical American, 12,* 25-43.

Center for Women Policy Studies. (1981). *Harassment and discrimination of women in employment.* Washington, D.C.: Author.

Cole, E. K. (1992). *Confronting sexual harassment and sexual violence in today's legal environment.* Unpublished paper. University of St. Thomas, St. Paul, MN.

Conte, A. (1990). *Sexual harassment in the workplace: Law and practice.* New York: John Wiley and Sons.

Dziech, B. W., & Weiner, L. (1984). *The lecherous professor.* Boston: Beacon Press.

Equal Employment Opportunity Commission. (1980). Guidelines in discrimination because of sex (Sect. 1604.11). *45 Federal Register 25024.*

Fitzgerald, L. F. (1990). Sexual harassment: The definition and management of a construct. In M.A. Paludi (Ed.), *Ivory power: Sexual harassment on campus.* Albany: SUNY Press.

Fitzgerald, L., Shullman, S., Bailey, N., Richards, M., Swecker, J., Gold, Y., Ormerod, M., & Weitzman, L. (1988). The incidence and dimensions of sexual harassment in academia and the workplace. *Journal of Vocational Behavior, 32,* 152-175.

Garber v. Saxon Business Products, 552 F.2d 1032 (4th Cir. 1977).

Gutek, B. (1985). *Sex and the workplace: The impact of sexual behavior and harassment on women, men, and organizations.* San Francisco: Jossey-Bass.

Harris v. Forklift Systems, Inc. 114 S. Ct. 367 (1993).

Heelan v. Johns-Manville Corp., 451 F. Supp. 459 (D. Mich. 1977).

Karasov, P. (1990, October 31). *University of St. Thomas sexual harassment training workshop.* Unpublished paper. St. Paul, MN.

Karsten, M. F., & Kramer, G. H. (1985). *Perceptions of sexual harassment in higher education.* Paper presented at the Women in Higher Education Conference, Orlando.

Maihoff, N., & Forrest, L. (1983). Sexual harassment in higher education: An assessment study. *Journal of the National Association of Women, Deans, Administrators and Counselors, 28,* 3-9.

Meritor Savings Bank v. Vinson, 477 U.S. 57 (1986).

Metha, A., & Nigg, J. (1983). Sexual harassment on campus: An institutional response. *Journal of the National Association of Women Deans, Administrators and Counselors, 46,* 9-15.

Paludi, M. (Ed.) (1990). *Ivory power: Sexual harassment on campus. Albany, NY: SUNY Press.*

Paludi, M., & Barickman, R. (1991). *Academic and workplace sexual harassment.* Albany, NY: SUNY Press.

Robertson, C., Dyer, C., & Campbell, D. (1985). *Report of survey of sexual harassment policies and procedures.* Bloomington: Indiana University, Office for Women's Affairs.

Ross, C. S., & Green, V. A. (1983). Sexual harassment: A liability higher education must face. *Journal of the College and University Personnel Association, 62,* 1-9.

Shank, B., & Johnston, N. (1986). *Sexual harassment: An issue for classroom and field educators.* Paper presented at the Annual Program Meeting of the Council on Social Work Education, Miami.

Title VII of the Civil Rights Act of 1964, 42 U.S.C. Sec. 2000e-2000-17.

Title IX of the Education Amendments of 1972, 20 U.S.C. Sec. 1681-1686.

Tomkins v. Public Service Electric & Gas Co., 568 F.2d 1044 (3rd Cir. 1977).

Whitmore, R. L. (1983). *Sexual harassment at UC Davis.* Davis, CA: University of California, Women's Resources and Research Center.

Wilson, K. R., & Kraus, L. A. (1983). Sexual harassment in the university. *Journal of College Student Personnel, 24,* 219-224.

2

Sexual Harassment in Graduate Schools of Social Work: Provocative Dilemmas

by Terry L. Singer

W hen one examines the dilemmas facing social work education today, reference frequently is made to the tensions between clinical and political dispositions, the decisions of professional commitments to targeted populations, and a range of other concerns regarding the role of social work in society. There is a tendency to consider these concerns when examining the development of curriculum content and standards, the students admitted to our schools, and the professional employment of our students. The schools truly are the gatekeepers of the profession and greatly influence the role of the profession in society.

One gatekeeping role that often is overlooked is the administration of the schools of social work. In this context, policies and procedures that reflect the values of the profession may present themselves as models or examples of professional behavior. This means that the treatment of students and faculty gives evidence of an internalized set of values. To paraphrase a question asked in an article on social workers in the workplace (Maypole, 1986), is it reasonable to expect that students, as future members of a profession that subscribes to high ideals, be treated with dignity and respect? One encounters dissonance if a school professes a belief in the dignity of the individual but operates according to policies or

Terry Singer is Dean of the School of Social Work, Marywood College.

An earlier version of this article was presented at the 1988 Council on Social Work Education Annual Program Meeting.

Reprinted from the *Journal of Social Work Education* (Winter 1989), with permission from CSWE.

procedures that disregard that belief. This paper examines one administrative function that reflects a larger societal issue—the management of personnel in relation to incidents of sexual harassment.

Major Social Issue

Stories abound about faculty who have disappeared quietly or found employment at other schools after being confronted with charges of sexual harassment of students. Sexual harassment has become a major social issue in recent days with the Supreme Court decision that considers it a breach of civil liberties. A book by Dziech and Weiner (1984), *The Lecherous Professor: Sexual Harassment on Campus*, and a national study by Robertson, Dyer, and Campbell (1985), have brought greater academic attention to a subject that conceptually is related to sexism, power, sex roles, sexuality, and other areas that pose provocative questions.

These questions point to the complexity of the sexual harassment issue. There is no common agreement on definitions for the concept (Reilly, Carpenter, Dull, & Bartlett, 1982; Somers, 1982; Wilson & Kraus, 1981; Weber-Burden & Rossi, 1982). An early attempt to define sexual harassment included such behaviors as verbal harassment, leering, offensive sexual remarks, unwanted touching, subtle pressure for sexual activity, overt demands for sexual activity, and physical assault ("Project on the Status and Education of Women," 1978). Many of those behaviors were included in the definitions for legal guidelines developed by the Equal Employment Opportunity Commission (1980) and used as the basis for institutional policies governing 75% of the colleges and universities with sexual harassment policies (Robertson, Dyer, & Campbell, 1985). Since the development of the EEOC guidelines in 1980, the courts have held that sexual harassment is a violation of Title VII of the Civil Rights Act, under which an administration can be held responsible if it fails to act when it knows or should know that an incident occurred (McCarthy, Ladimer, & Sirefman, 1984). Although some authors claim that confusion of definition is a "transparent pretense" (Dziech & Weiner, 1984), others, such as Anne Truax, Director of the Women's Center at the University of Minnesota, report that there is often little disagreement between student and professor about the actual behavior, but there is a difference of interpretation or assignment of meaning (Fitzgerald, 1986).

An often cited topic that points to differences of opinion on the subject is the consensual sexual activity between student and professor. Such a situation creates a gray area for interpretation and sanction. Some civil libertarians argue that consenting adults have the freedom of choice. The real threats of harassment get clouded under this veil of confusion (Fitzgerald, 1986; Heller, 1986; Schneider, 1987). Some studies indicate that problems may occur once the relationship between the two consenting adults begins to break down. Regardless of what some may claim, the problem does not involve legislating morality; rather, as Robertson, Dyer, and Campbell (1985) explain:

> . . . under the law, it is not the sexual conduct itself which is prohibited, but the discriminatory and damaging impact it can have within the special relationship of trust between teacher and student. (p. 9)

Because of the problems inherent in all forms of sexual activity between faculty and student, some institutions, like the University of Iowa, have adopted policies that prohibit sexual harassment and amorous, consensual relations between faculty and students.

Extent of the Problem

Although an accurate accounting of sexual harassment is difficult to pinpoint, there is some evidence to suggest that the problem is widespread. The Robertson, Dyer, and Campbell (1985) study indicates that only 37% of institutions keep statistics on the number of complaints. Despite this small percentage, their survey also suggests that 20% to 30% of all female students experience some form of sexual harassment every year, but only 2% to 3% of them are likely to report anything. This incidence rate is supported by other studies. Further, 65% of complaints made are submitted to deans. These figures are for undergraduate students and may be higher for female graduate students.

Research studies that factor out undergraduate and graduate student experiences with sexual harassment are still few, but several of them characterize a serious problem for graduate female students (Fitzgerald, 1986; Schneider, 1987). In the Schneider report, 60% of the research sample reported at least one experience of harassment by male faculty during graduate school. Twenty-two percent had been asked out socially by a male faculty member; nearly two-thirds of them accepted. Heller (1986) reports that one-third of all female holders of doctorates in psychology reported unwarranted sexual advances by faculty, and that many of these advances came from research advisers. Schneider has painted a picture suggesting that graduate students are victimized more often than undergraduates are because they are closer in age and experience to faculty members. At the same time, they are more dependent than undergraduates for career support such as doctoral admission, grades, accommodations, committee memberships, and financial and research opportunities. These necessary supports often provide leverage points for the introduction of harassment possibilities.

Frequently, the suggestion is made, as it is in rape cases, that the victim actually may be a disgruntled student or jilted lover, and is making false claims. In actuality, false claims appear to be minimal. In the study by Robertson, Dyer, and Campbell (1985), it was reported that 82% of the institutions received no false complaints, and that most schools that did report false claims had just one. Their data further suggest that false complaints account for less than 1% of charges annually.

The current literature is clear in documenting a widespread social problem. Best estimates are that at least one-third of all female students are harassed, sometimes causing very serious consequences for the victim and the larger community.

Consequences of the Problem

There are many consequences of sexual harassment in colleges and universities. First, a large percentage of victims are affected emotionally. The result may be impaired social relationships (Maypole, 1986), or worse, an experience resembling that of rape victims who engage in torturous self-blame or suffer the blame of others (Garvey, 1986). In addition, many of these victims live in fear of retaliation in the belief that no help is available.

Another result of the phenomenon is the increased financial burden of lawsuits. Although most cases of sexual harassment do not end up in the courts, and although there is little documentation as to the number of colleges involved in civil suits, there is evidence from business to demonstrate the expense of legal suits for both business and victim (Robertson, Dyer, & Campbell, 1985).

A third consequence of sexual harassment has been the development and employment of strong statements of policy and procedure against such behavior. The research is beginning to conclude that such statements represent the best protection for colleges and universities, and may even prevent incidents from occurring (Robertson, Dyer, & Campbell, 1985; Young, 1985; "Suggested Policy," 1983).

Reportedly two-thirds of colleges and universities have written sexual harassment policies, and 46% have grievance procedures for sexual harassment complaints (Robertson, Dyer, & Campbell, 1985). The presence of these policies and procedures tends to correlate positively with institutional size.

A final result of sexual harassment within social institutions may point to a serious social problem of sustained gender stratification. Hoffman (1986) has written:

> . . . uncritical tolerance of sexual harassment has perpetuated inequality between men and women, reinforced the sexual objectification of women, and encouraged the privatization of relationships which exploit economic and cultural inequality for sexual gain. (p. 116)

This problem tears at the social fabric and may pose the most serious threat of all.

Social work, as a profession, has had a long-standing commitment to issues of oppression and powerlessness. Its history is rich in advocacy for equality, rights of self-determination, and the inherent dignity and worth of the individual. As indicated at the beginning of this article, it is important to display those values within schools of social work, and within the context of beginning socialization to the profession. Failure to do so could conceivably undermine the early professional base. Thus, this paper reports on a national survey of the deans and directors of schools of social work to explore the extent and nature of the problem of sexual harassment, and to establish an understanding of how schools deal with the problem.

Research Methodology

The study consisted of a one group design, which is considered descriptive research. This study addressed the following questions:

a) What are the demographic characteristics of current graduate programs of social work?

b) What are the characteristics of those accused of sexual harassment and of the victims of harassment?

c) Are there any institutional characteristics that are related to the ways in which cases of sexual harassment are managed within schools of social work?

d) Are there any demographic characteristics of social work programs that are related to experiences with sexual harassment?

The information to address these questions included demographic data, deans and directors' (from this point identified as deans) actual reports of sexual harassment, and data concerning disposition of cases. The definition of sexual harassment was determined by the institution or school, and not by any specific behavioral criterion.

The sexual harassment survey was developed and mailed to 99 deans of graduate programs of social work in Spring 1987. This number represented all of the accredited Masters' degree graduate programs. A cover letter was attached urging response and indicating the importance of developing a base to begin understanding of this timely issue. After one month, a follow-up letter and another copy of the questionnaire were sent to those who had not replied. A total of 83 deans and directors completed and returned questionnaires, constituting a very high response rate of 84%. Data collection occurred during a three-month period.

The data from the questionnaires initially were analyzed using descriptive statistics. Associations and relationships among a number of variables were analyzed using chi-square and Pearson Correlation. Significance was accepted at the .05 level of probability.

Results

Demographic Characteristics

Considering the size of return and using comparable variables of institutional size, MSW population, and faculty size, there are no significant factors to suggest that the sample is not representative (*Statistics on Social Work Education*, 1987). As seen in Table 1, most institutions have a specific institutional policy on sexual harassment (89%), and a grievance procedure specifically for sexual harassment (69%). Only 8% of the social work units report having their own policy, and only 12% have their own grievance procedures separate from the institution.

Reports of Sexual Harassment

Schools that have been involved with problems of sexual harassment typically have been confronted with information in several ways. Fifty-four percent of the surveyed social work programs have had reports of sexual harassment during the years 1984–1989. Of the 45 confronted with the problem, harassment was reported directly to the dean by the victim in 10 cases. In 15 cases the dean heard directly from the victim and indirectly from others, whereas in 20

Table 1. Demographic Data on Accredited MSW Programs

Item	Categories	Number	%
Institutional Size	1,000–3,999	7	9
	4,000–7,999	6	8
	8,000–11,999	10	13
	12,000–19,999	21	26
	20,000+	36	45
MSW Student Population	Mean	264	
	Standard deviation	173.73	
Full-time Faculty	Mean	21	
	Standard deviation	9.58	
Part-time Faculty	Mean	12	
	Standard deviation	13.92	
Field Supervisors	Mean	140	
	Standard deviation	92.93	
Staff	Mean	12	
	Standard deviation	10.56	
Institutions with Sexual	Yes	74	89
Harassment Policy	No	9	11
Institutions with Sexual	Yes	52	69
Harassment Grievance	No	23	31
Procedures	Missing Data	8	
Social Work Programs with	Yes	7	9
Sexual Harassment Policy	No	75	91
	Missing Data	1	
Social Work Programs with	Yes	10	12
Sexual Harassment	No	72	88
Grievance Procedures	Missing data	1	

$N = 83$

cases only indirect reports reached the dean. Most (41) of these schools had two or fewer accused harassers.

Characteristics of Victims and Those Accused

The deans were asked to profile the victims and those accused of sexual harassment in cases where the report of abuse came directly from the victim, under the assumption that deans would be most likely to have complete information when the victim came forward. The respondents identified 39 faculty and field supervisors in social work programs who were accused of sexual harassment in complaints made to the dean in 25 different institutions (Table 2). Those charged tended to be senior male faculty, averaging age 46. Twenty-three of the accused harassers had only one complaint lodged against them, although 10 had four or more complaints.

The data on victims are not as complete as data on those charged. There was one report of a male victim of male faculty harassment,

Table 2. Profile of Those Accused of Sexual Harassment and Disposition of Cases when Victim Reported Directly to Dean

Item	Categories	Number
School Status	Faculty	23
	Field Supervisor	8
	Missing Data	8
Faculty Rank	Full Professor	11
(where applicable)	Associate Professor	7
	Assistant Professor	2
	Missing Data	11
Sex	Male	31
	Female	0
	Missing Data	8
Number of Complaints	Mean	2.7
per accused	Standard Deviation	3.3
	Mode/Median	0.0
Formal Grievance	Yes	9
Filed	No	26
	Missing Data	4
Formal Grievance	Dismissal of Charges	2
Disposition	Reprimand	4
	Dismissed	1
	Missing Data	2
Disposition of Cases	No Action	12
with no Formal	Dismissal of Charges	1
Grievance	Reprimand	6
	Resignation	1
	Current Review	1
	Missing Data	5

$N = 39$

but the majority of victims were female. Fifty-five victims were identified for 29 of the accused harassers. The average age of the victims was 28 years.

It is important to remember when reading this data that it only reflects those cases that were made known directly to the dean by the victim.

Response to Sexual Harassment

There was a wide range of disposition of cases filed to the deans by victims. Nine of those charged with sexual harassment had formal grievances filed by the victims (Table 2). In two cases, the reviewing committee recommended a dismissal of charges; in four cases reprimands were recommended; and in one case dismissal was recommended. Even when there had been no formal grievance, action was taken in some cases. Twelve of the accused had no grievances filed; six were reprimanded, and one resigned. In one case charges were dismissed, and one was under review. There were only two reports of litigation. One suit brought by a victim was settled out of court, and the other suit brought against the college by the faculty member was still pending. These findings were based on charges being initiated in the dean's office directly by those who claimed to be victims of sexual harassment. It is not clear from reading the results of cases with no formal grievance what the category "No Action" meant. Possibly, cases may have been unfounded or ignored. Because these are cases with no formal grievances, perhaps an unwillingness to follow through by the victim resulted in the response of No Action. In addition, the fact that only one charge was dismissed strengthens the notion that the category No Action may overlap with this category.

Charges of harassment brought to deans indirectly rather than by the victim may have included reports by other students, administrators, faculty, field work representatives, or others. Most deans took some type of action on the indirect information: 21 cases were followed up with direct discussion, and in seven an investigation was initiated. In nine cases no information was available and in only four cases was the charge ignored as rumor. In several cases, deans' responses varied, depending upon the information received. For example, one dean ignored one complaint while following up another with direct discussion.

The questionnaire contained an open-ended question to discover the disposition of complaints made indirectly to deans. Although it was not possible to quantify responses accurately, there clearly were two dispositions that stood out. The most frequently mentioned situation involved the victims' refusal to follow through with the complaint. This may explain why complaints were not made directly to the dean by the victim. The literature reflects dynamics of fear and concern for retaliation as reasons for this response (Robertson, Dyer, & Campbell, 1985). The second most frequently mentioned response was mutual resolution by the parties involved. In some cases the accused was directed to stay away from the victim and she was accommodated by not having to maintain contact with the harasser.

Program Characteristics in Relation to Sexual Harassment

This study is guided in part by a question of relationships that might exist between demographics and reported experiences of

Table 3. Relationship of Selected Variables to Schools Reporting Sexual Harassment Problems

	Reports of Sexual Harassment	No Reports of Sexual Harassment	
Institutional Sexual Harassment Policy	41	33	$\chi^2 = 8.86$ $df = 1$ $N = 82$
No Institutional Sexual Harassment Policy	0	8	$p = .0029$
School Sexual Harassment Policy	6	1	$\chi^2 = 3.65$ $df = 1$ $N = 80$
No School Sexual Harassment Policy	35	38	$p = .0562$
Institutional Grievance Procedures for Sexual Harassment	30	22	$\chi^2 = 2.82$ $df = 1$ $N = 74$
No Institutional Grievance Procedures for Sexual Harassment	8	14	$p = .0934$
School Grievance Procedures for Sexual Harassment	7	3	$\chi^2 = 1.94$ $df = 1$ $N = 81$
No School Grievance Procedures for Sexual Harassment	33	38	$p = .1637$
Public Institution	27	28	$\chi^2 = .07$ $df = 1$ $N = 79$
Private Institution	11	13	$p = .7898$
Religious Institution	3	6	$\chi^2 = 3.76$ $df = 1$ $N = 27$
Non-Sectarian Institution	13	5	$p = .0525$

sexual harassment. Chi-square test of independence was computed for selected variables on the basis of suggestions of possible relationships found in a review of the literature. The results of these analyses are stated in Table 3.

These results suggest that those institutions with a policy against sexual harassment are more likely to report sexual harassment. A policy may give a message to faculty, staff, and students that action will be taken if reported. There was also a tendency towards significance for schools with their own policies against harassment to report sexual harassment charges ($p = .05$). This may simply parallel the effect of the previous point that students may expect action where policies are in place.

The presence of grievance *procedures* to manage sexual harassment complaints does not seem to be related to reporting of abuse. Nor does the public-private school designation affect reporting. Non-sectarian institutions tended to report more harassment than religious institutions ($p = .05$). However, the n was small because most schools did not report religious affiliation.

Several other variables were analyzed using Pearson Correlation to examine relationships to number of reports of sexual harassment. None of these correlations proved to be significant: Size of the institution, number of MSW students, number of full-time faculty, number of part-time faculty, number of staff, and the number of agency field supervisors.

Perceived Role of CSWE

Asked what role should be played by the Council on Social Work Education in response to the issue of sexual harassment, 24 deans believed there is no role for the Council, reflecting primarily a strong belief in the concept of institutional autonomy in handling institutional problems. A number of deans (12) did indicate, however, that CSWE might play an educational or consultative role in keeping this important issue before the schools. Seventeen believed it should recommend procedures and two added that it should develop an official position. Eleven deans went so far as to suggest an active monitoring role for the Council, similar to other areas monitored through accreditation reviews.

Summary

The survey of deans and directors of MSW programs has pointed to a serious problem of sexual harassment with 54% of programs indicating reports of such behavior over the years 1984–1989. Most of this behavior seems to be directed towards young women by senior faculty, although a quarter of the reports concern field supervisors. Students from large schools may be more willing to report such abuse directly to the dean, but overwhelmingly, the complaints come to the dean by other sources. Institutions need to be sensitive to the seriousness of speaking out about one's victimization, particularly for graduate students, who rely so heavily on faculty for career support.

There is some evidence to suggest that the implementation of institutional policies and grievance procedures directed at the problems of sexual harassment may be related to high numbers of reports. The literature suggests that the presence of policies and procedures sends a message that sexual harassment will not be tolerated (Robertson, Dyer, & Campbell, 1985; Young, 1985; "Suggested Policy," 1983). This is the likeliest interpretation, although one cannot rule out the possibility that institutions have developed such processes in response to reports of abuse. It also is interesting to note that recent data on the number of institutions reporting policies and procedures appear to indicate a rise since the study of Robertson, Dyer, and Campbell reported 67% and 46%, respectively; in this 1989 study, the percentages are 89% and 69%. Perhaps the subject has come of age.

Limitations to this study are rather obvious. First, little research has been done to establish baseline data or clear methodologies that point to the gathering of accurate data. Even though the questionnaire was pre-tested there were unanticipated responses that made categorization of the data difficult.

Second, deans may report data inaccurately either to protect the reputation of the school or to politicize the issue more dramatically. The gender of the dean may affect the interpretation or representation of the data, although it should be pointed out that there is no evidence to suggest that any such bias exists. It certainly is an area for further study.

Informal follow-up with deans to discuss these findings established clear feelings of concern by the deans about the extent of the problem and the sometimes ambiguous follow-through. The deans are challenged by the precepts of the profession to take a much more aggressive posture in relation to the issue of sexual harassment. Perhaps the deans could initiate more educational input to helping students, faculty, and field supervisors understand the related issues and policies. Furthermore, in colleges and universities where policies against sexual harassment have not been articulated, deans could give leadership to that development.

The Council on Social Work Education also should be challenged by these results to take a strong role. Even though the deans generally do not want CSWE to interfere with institutional matters, it is possible that the Council could give more leadership and direction by providing guidelines, consultation, and education. This could be supported by clearer and stronger resolutions of the National Association of Social Workers to direct efforts against sexual harassment in schools of social work.

This study is only an early attempt to explore the problem and scope of sexual harassment in schools of social work. The study raises more questions than answers. It also raises the specter of concern: What assurances are professional schools making that social work values are being modeled in the classroom? The data of this study suggest the need for careful scrutiny of attitudes and behaviors to assess the selection of faculty and field supervisors in particular. Also, deans, institutions, schools of social work, CSWE, and NASW need to be the recourse against such abusive behaviors. Only through comprehensive diligence can the profession make progress against the instruments of destruction that undermine the professional base of practice and the social fabric as a whole.

References

Dziech, B. W., & Weiner, L. (1984). *The lecherous professor: Sexual harassment on campus.* Boston: Beacon Press.

Equal Employment Opportunity Commission. (1980). *Sexual harassment guidelines.* (29 CFR, CHAPTER XIV, Part 1604.11(a). Washington, D.C.: U.S. Government Printing Office.

Fitzgerald, K. (1986). Sexual blackmail: Schools get serious about harassment. *MS, 15,* 24.

Garvey, M. (1986). The high cost of sexual harassment suits. *Personnel Journal, 65*(1), 75-80.

Heller, S. (1986). 1 in 6 female students in psychology reports having sexual contact with a professor. *Chronicle of Higher Education, 31,* 23.

Hoffman, F. L. (1986). Sexual harassment in academia: Feminist theory and institutional practice. *Harvard Educational Review, 56*(2), 105-121.

Jensen, I. W., & Gutek, B. A. (1982). Attributions and assignments of responsibility in sexual harassment. *Journal of Social Issues, 38*(4), 121-136.

Maypole, D. E. (1986). Sexual harassment of social workers at work: Injustice within? *Social Work, 31*(1), 29-34.

McCarthy, J., Ladimer, I., & Sirefman, J. P. (1984). *Managing faculty disputes.* San Francisco: Jossey-Bass, Inc.

Project on the Status and Education of Women (1978). *Sexual Harassment.* Washington, D.C.: Association of American Colleges.

Reilly, T., Carpenter, S., Dull, V., & Bartlett, K. (1982). The factorial survey: An approach to defining sexual harassment on campus. *Journal of Social Issues, 38*(4), 99-110.

Robertson, C., Dyer, C., & Campbell, D. (1985). Report on survey of sexual harassment policies and procedures. (Report prepared by the Office for Women's Affairs) Bloomington: Indiana University.

Schneider, B. E. (1987). Graduate women, sexual harassment and university policy. *The Journal of Higher Education, 58*(1), 46-65.

Somers, A. (1982). Sexual harassment in academe: Legal issues and definitions. *Journal of Social Issues, 38*(4), 23-32.

Statistics on Social Work Education in the United States: 1986. (1987). Washington, D.C.: Council on Social Work Education.

Suggested policy and procedures for handling complaints. (1983). *Academe,* 15a-16a.

Weber-Burden, E., & Rossi, P. H. (1982). Defining sexual harassment on campus: A replication and extension. *Journal of Social Issues, 38*(4), 111-120.

Wilson, K., & Kraus, L. (1981). *Sexual harassment in the university.* Paper presented to the Annual Meeting of the American Sociological Association, Toronto.

Young, D. P. (1985). Legal issues. *ACAFAD, 10*(3).

3

Sexual Harassment in Social Work Field Placements

by Deborah Valentine, John Gandy, Caroline Burry, and Leon Ginsberg

S exual harassment in the workplace is well documented and pervasive. Statistics indicate that anywhere from 42% to 90% of women will experience some form of harassment during their employed lives (Hill, 1992). *NASW News*, in an article entitled "Agencies No Haven" (1984), reported that social workers are not immune to sexual harassment. Over one-third of the female respondents and one-seventh of the male respondents to this NASW-member survey had experienced some kind of sexual harassment in the workplace.

Sexual harassment of college students has also been an issue of concern. Since the 1970s, student vulnerability to sexual harassment—due to fear of faculty reprisals such as lowered grades or denied recommendations—has been discussed by academic administrators. In addition, from 28% to 33% of surveyed students have reported experiencing some form of sexual harassment, as defined by the researcher (Roscoe, Goodwin, Repp, & Rose, 1987). It could be argued, however, that rates would be higher if students were allowed to define sexual harassment themselves.

As a result of concerns about sexually harassing behavior, definitions of sexual harassment and laws prohibiting sexual harassment have emerged in both the workplace and academic settings. Furthermore, universities and places of employment are now liable if they fail to adequately handle complaints of sexual harassment.

Although the majority of sexual harassment incidents go unreported (Roscoe et al., 1987), many employees are protected by law in

Deborah Valentine is Associate Professor, John Gandy is Associate Dean, Caroline Burry is a Doctoral Student, and Leon Ginsberg is Research Professor at the College of Social Work, University of South Carolina.

the workplace, and students are protected in the classroom. It is doubtful, however, whether all students in field placements are protected from sexual harassment. University policies on sexual harassment, for example, typically refer only to sexual harassment by paid employees; thus, agency-based field supervisors and personnel may be excluded. Furthermore, students are frequently excluded from mention in the sexual harassment policies of social service agencies either because they are not paid employees or because no sexual harassment policy exists. Because sexual harassment or any form of harassment interferes with a student's ability to learn, social work educators must be attentive to the potential for sexual harassment in social work field settings.

This chapter reviews the critical issues pertaining to sexual harassment as they apply to social work students in their field placements, and reports on the results of a nationwide survey of graduate schools of social work. The vulnerabilities of students in field placements are identified and the roles of social work administrators, field instructors, and college administrators in the prevention of sexual harassment are addressed. In addition, this chapter reviews commonalities in policies specifically protecting students in field placements, provides a sexual harassment policy developed by the University of South Carolina for social work students in field placement (Appendix B), and suggests the means for implementing a comprehensive sexual harassment policy specifically designed for social work students in field placement.

Historical, Legal, and Regulatory Base

The Workplace

The hostile work environment theory, now used in sexual harassment cases, was first introduced in a discrimination claim based on national origin in 1972. In *N. Jay Rogers v. EEOC,* a woman with a Spanish surname charged that her work environment at an optometrist's office was offensive because of the employer's policy of segregating patients. The court held that even though this employment practice was not directly aimed at the employee, the relationship between employees and their workplace is so significant that employees' psychological well-being, as well as their economic benefits, are statutorily entitled to protection from employer abuse under Section 703, Title VII of the 1964 Civil Rights Act. *Rogers* states, in part: "One can readily envision working environments so heavily polluted with discrimination as to destroy completely the emotional and psychological stability of minority group workers" (p. 238). Thus, a claim of hostile work environment may refer not only to racially or ethnically offensive conduct directed at the employee, but to behavior or policies that create an atmosphere that is demeaning to an employee. The court further maintained that the damage need not be a tangible or monetary loss; it could be the undermining of the individual's well-being. Finally, the court recognized that employment discrimination does not always take the form of "a series of isolated and distinguishable events," but is sometimes manifested by "a complex and pervasive phenomenon" (p. 238).

The Equal Employment Opportunity Commission (EEOC), the federal agency charged with investigating and mediating discrimination cases under Title VII of the 1964 Civil Rights Act, has had an important role in addressing sexual harassment in the workplace. By 1977, three cases charging sexual harassment were argued at the appellate level and established that a harassed person had the right to sue the corporate entity that employed her or him (Brownmiller & Alexander, 1992). By 1980, Eleanor Holmes Norton, chair of the EEOC under the Carter administration, issued guidelines stating that sexual activity as a condition of employment or promotion was a violation of Title VII. She also made it clear that the creation of an intimidating, hostile, or offensive working environment was also a violation, and that verbal abuse was deemed sufficient to create a hostile environment. The guidelines encouraged corporations to develop their own policies and inform employees of appropriate means for redress (Pollack, 1990).

It was not until 1986, however, that the Supreme Court affirmed unanimously in *Meritor Savings Bank v. Vinson* that *sexual harassment* without economic harm was considered unlawful discrimination, and that a hostile or abusive work environment may constitute sexual harassment under Title VII. Five years later, in *L. Robinson v. Jacksonville Shipyards* (1991), U.S. District Judge Howell Melton ruled that pictures of nude and semi-nude women displayed in the workplace are a form of sexual harassment. Melton found that women are affected by "sex role spillover," in which their evaluation was based more on sexual worth than on their performance. Title VII also states that a claim of unintentional harassment is not allowed as an employer defense. Furthermore, employers are liable for the actions of their agents or representatives (employees) in cases where the supervisory chain knew or should have known of the misconduct (Scott, 1988).

Academic Settings

Sexual harassment of students by faculty members has received increased attention by college and university administrators in the last several years. In the 1979 case of *Cannon v. University of Chicago*, the Supreme Court established that an individual has a private right of action and can file a private lawsuit against an educational institution for sex discrimination on the basis of Title IX of the 1972 Education Amendments. Before these early cases of litigation involving sexual harassment of students, guidance for university administrators in developing and implementing sexual harassment policies had been limited. Eventually, these cases established that, for educational institutions receiving federal assistance, sexual harassment of students is considered sex discrimination.

The national Advisory Council on Women's Educational Programs formulated the following working definition of sexual harassment:

> Academic sexual harassment is the use of authority to emphasize the sexuality or sexual identity of a student in a manner which prevents or impairs that student's full enjoyment of educational benefits, climate or opportunities. (Till, 1980, p. 7)

The Council found that five types of activities were described as sexual harassment:

1. Generalized sexist remarks or behavior;
2. Inappropriate and offensive but essentially sanction-free sexual advances;
3. Solicitation of sexual activity or other sex-linked behavior by promise of rewards;
4. Coercion of sexual activity by threat of punishment; or
5. Sexual assaults. (Polakoff, 1984)

A 1981 memorandum from the U.S. Department of Education reiterated that sexual harassment of students violates Title IX and that universities are liable if they fail to deal adequately with student complaints of sexual harassment (Perry, 1983). Whether or not a grievance procedure exists within a college or university, students may take complaints of sexual harassment directly to the Office for Civil Rights in the Department of Education or press charges in a private lawsuit. Grievance procedures within colleges and universities, however, have the potential to be more responsive to complaints of sexual harassment. Courts and the Office for Civil Rights have been extremely slow in adjudicating complaints of sexual harassment (Brandenburg, 1982).

Problem Background

Pervasiveness of Sexual Harassment

The pervasiveness of sexual harassment is undeniable. In a survey of 23,100 employees conducted by the U.S. Merit System Protection Board in 1980, more than 40% of female federal employees and 15% of male employees reported experiencing sexual harassment on the job in the previous two years (Blonston & Scanlan, 1991). *Redbook*'s survey of its readers in 1976 reported the highest incidence of all studies: 88% of the 9,000 respondents reported that they had experienced some form of sexual harassment at work (Coles, 1986).

In the academic arena, researchers at the University of California at Berkeley surveyed 290 female graduate students in 1977 and reported that one in five believed that she had been harassed by male teachers (Craib, 1977). In a study at Cornell University, 92% of the female respondents listed sexual harassment as a serious problem and 70% reported having personally experienced it in some form (MacKinnon, 1979).

Schneider (1987) reported the results from a questionnaire completed by 356 female graduate students representing 43 departments. Overall, 60% reported experiencing sexual harassment by male faculty during their graduate careers. One student wrote:

> Most of the abuse I know of . . . is verbal. Jokes in the classroom and hallway which are sexist; remarks which put down women. Sexist behavior in the sense of acting out traditional sex roles is rampant at the school and the faculty are the worst offenders. (p. 51)

Another student wrote:

> I was in a course with a teacher who frequently physically objectified women and told rape jokes in class. Watching his interactions with other women students, and the male bonding with his rape jokes, had a serious negative impact on my academic performance. I was angry in class. I skipped numerous of his classes. It had a definite negative psychological impact on my well-being. I will never take another course from him. In repeating my feelings and experiences to male graduate students about

this faculty member, the general response was that I took him and the situation too seriously, that he was basically a "nice guy." I would leave class or these discussions hardly able to see straight with frustration and fury. (Schneider, 1987, p. 52)

In a unique study by Fitzgerald, Weitzman, Gold, and Ormerod (1988), 235 male faculty members were asked to respond to a survey inquiring about social and sexual interaction among faculty and students. Over 37% of the sample indicated that they had attempted to initiate personal relationships with students; over 25% indicated that they had dated students; around 26% reported that they had engaged in sexual encounters or relations with students; and 11% indicated that they had attempted to stroke, caress, or touch female students. Despite these responses, only *one* subject reported that he believed he had ever sexually harassed a student. Six percent, however, believed that they had been sexually harassed by their female students.

Consequences of Sexual Harassment

Data from recent studies such as those cited make it clear that sexual harassment in the workplace or in academic settings is not uncommon. The consequences of sexual harassment for victims and the organizations in which they work or attend school are serious. Research suggests that sexual harassment has a variety of negative effects on victims. Kaplan (1991) reports that an "overwhelming majority of victims experienced changes in affect and many developed physical problems as a consequence of the harassment" (p. 53). Negative emotional reactions can affect women's performance on their jobs: women report less ambition, less job satisfaction, and impaired job performance as a result of experiencing sexual harassment (Kaplan, 1991). Research indicates that the majority of women handle sexual harassment primarily by behaving passively—ignoring the behavior and avoiding the harasser. According to Livingston (1982), ignoring the behavior often results in continued harassment. Kaplan (1991) states: "The price that individuals paid in negative affect, somatization, and negative attitudes toward work were passed on to their employers through absenteeism, increased medical claims, and reduced productivity" (p. 54).

Despite sexual harassment policies in many organizations and academic settings, most women do not report incidents of harassment. The Merit Systems Protection Board revealed that only 2% of the employees who experienced sexual harassment filed complaints, and only half of these believed that their complaints were successful. Employees who did not file complaints explained that they doubted a complaint would resolve the problem (Blonston & Scanlan, 1991). Adams, Kottke, and Padgitt (1983) sent questionnaires to 1,000 graduate and undergraduate students. They reported that many students did not know the procedure for reporting instances of sexual harassment, and that victims of sexual harassment suffered physical aches, ailments, reduced ability to concentrate, lessened ambition and self-confidence, sleeplessness, depression, and disillusionment with male faculty members. In a study of university students conducted by Roscoe et al. (1987), only 4% knew which university office handled incidents of sexual harassment. Schneider (1987) reports from one student:

> I think when I came to graduate school I was incredibly naive. I wish I had reported the first incident. I was afraid to. He was my instructor for the toughest course in the program, and he might have denied it or said he was only kidding. I was afraid of embarrassing myself by having it get around. I was afraid of being involved in a scandal the first thing in graduate school. I didn't know anyone here and did not know who even to report to. I had no friends here. . . . I felt my innocence, trust and loneliness were taken advantage of. . . . Another reason I did not take action: I tend to be afraid of conflict and nonassertive; I don't really like this, but it's how I was brought up. (pp. 57-58)

Sexual Harassment in Social Work Field Placements

A thorough review of the literature reveals no data pertaining to the extent, pervasiveness, or kind of sexual harassment that students in internships and field placements experience, despite the importance of internships in medicine, nursing, teacher education, occupational therapy, physical therapy, and other fields. Given the extent of sexual harassment in work and educational settings and the fact that student interns have little power and multiple vulnerabilities, it is probable that those in field placement settings suffer high rates of sexual harassment. Several illustrations of sexual harassment in social work field placement settings, drawn from actual incidents, follow.

Illustration 1. Within two weeks of starting her placement in a large residential treatment center for adolescents, a first-year social work student was asked by the director of child care workers to come to his home to discuss the teenage residents. Because she felt uncomfortable visiting the director at his home and had no interest in pursuing a social relationship with him, the student told her field instructor about the situation. The social work field supervisor suggested that she find a way to handle the situation herself. The student decided to refuse the requests of the director and deliberately become more formal with him. The week following her conference with the field instructor, the director called her home and left a sexually explicit message on her answering machine. The student immediately notified her field instructor and field liaison.

Illustration 2. A second-year social work student was working in a substance abuse field placement. The mid-term evaluation conference between the field instructor, field liaison, and student went well. The field instructor reported that he felt that the student was developing mastery of advanced social work practice skills and that her progress was satisfactory; the student reported that she was comfortable in the placement, that her learning needs were being met, and that supervision was going well. The next Monday morning, the student reported to the field liaison that during a weekend agency retreat, her field instructor "grabbed, hugged, and kissed" her. She felt she could no longer return to the field placement and never wanted to see her field instructor again. The field liaison called the field instructor, who admitted his behavior but indicated that it was nothing more than a "friendly and supportive" gesture that the student had misinterpreted. The field liaison supported the student, helping her to explore options for a new field placement and for pressing charges. A conference was scheduled with the director of field placements, the field liaison, and the student. However, on the day before this conference, the student withdrew from the social work program.

Illustration 3. A female social work graduate student was working in a community care home for young adults with mental retardation for her first-year field placement. Throughout her first semester, she experienced extensive social and sexual harassment from her field supervisor. For example, he would talk about the big penises of the male clients and, during lunch hour, he would ask the student to give him detailed reports of the sexual histories of her clients. Because of the power he had in the agency and over her, she decided to complete the semester. The field supervisor wrote a positive semester evaluation of her work, and, after the evaluation was signed, the student informed him that she wanted to work in a different unit of the agency, under the guidance of another field supervisor. The supervisor became enraged, yelling at and insulting her. Shortly thereafter, he told her field liaison that although she'd been given every opportunity to learn about the field of mental retardation, the student was not cut out for the stress and difficulty of working with this population. He had recommended that she pass the semester, but he no longer wanted her in the agency.

Although the pervasiveness of sexual harassment in field placement settings is unknown, the above real-life examples illustrate the need for policies to protect students and to inform field liaisons, field supervisors, and others involved in field placements. One important question that must be answered is whether social work students in field placements are protected by existing policies on sexual harassment. While most universities have policies that protect students in the classroom, more information is needed about policies that specifically cover students in field placements. This study attempts to provide such information by presenting data from a national survey of MSW programs in the United States.

Methodology

A survey, in the form of a postcard, was used to collect information from MSW programs. The postcard stated the intent of the study—to determine if graduate schools of social work have specific policies to protect social work students from sexual harassment in their field placements—and posed two yes-no questions. The first question asked if the school has a sexual harassment policy that protects students in the academic setting; the second asked if the school has a sexual harassment policy that protects students in their field placement settings. Respondents were requested to send copies of their sexual harassment policies for students in the field. In June 1991, the postcards were mailed to all CSWE-accredited MSW programs (n = 108). Responses were received from 73 programs, yielding a return rate of 68%. Sexual harassment policies were received from 22 programs.

Results

The postcard survey findings are presented in Table 1 on the following page.

Table 1. The Presence of a Sexual Harassment Policy

Variable	Yes		No	
	No.	%	No.	%
School reports sexual harassment policy that protects students in academic settings	66	90%	7	10%
School reports sexual harassment policy that protects students in field placement*	23	32%	49	68%

* Although 73 postcard surveys were returned, one did not indicate whether or not the school has a sexual harassment policy that specifically protects students in field placement.

Of the schools that responded, 66 (90%) reported having a sexual harassment policy protecting students in the academic setting, and 23 (32%) reported having a sexual harassment policy specifically protecting students in field placements. Of the 22 sexual harassment policies sent by respondents, only 8 actually contained language related to students in field settings. Nine of the 22 respondents who returned policies added notes indicating a presumption that their program's sexual harassment policy would apply to MSW students in their field placements. Eight of the 22 respondents who returned policies stated categorically that their program's policy protected students in field placements. However, of the 8 policies that mentioned the protection of students in field placement, 4 were brief, vague, and rather nonspecific; gave little consideration to process and procedure, examples, and resolution; and seemed to be based on an academic rather than field placement model. A respondent who had returned one such policy attached a note with this concern:

> I expect that we would follow these guidelines as closely as we could should an allegation of sexual harassment occur in field placement. In fact, however, our field manual does not include any discussion of sexual harassment and, thus, there is really no way for field instructors to know what the University policy is.... I believe we need to consider whether to extend the policy formally to the field instruction setting.

Although there were some differences, primarily in length and detail, a number of commonalities were found among the four policies that clearly and specifically protected students.

1. Introductory statement
   a. Specific policy to protect social work students from sexual harassment in field placements
   b. Why it is an important issue in a professional school
2. Definition
   a. Specific and inclusive
   b. Discussion of individuals who may be involved
   c. Examples of what sexual harassment can include (threats, suggestions, behavior, comments, and physical contact)
3. Procedures
   a. Responsibilities of the student
   b. Responsibilities of the director of field, field faculty, and agency personnel
   c. Responsibilities of the dean or director of the school
   d. Investigation process
4. Resolution
5. Consensual relationships
6. Use of field agencies
   a. Sexual harassment policy in the agency
   b. School's sexual harassment policy distributed to field agencies and instructors

Judging by the responses to this survey, there is a widespread assumption that university sexual harassment policies cover field placements as well as academic settings. The unique nature of student field placements, however, raises serious questions about this assumption. It appears that students are probably *not* protected by university policies, because universities cannot compel any other agency or entity to comply with their internal policies. Furthermore, it is unclear whether field students are protected by sexual harassment policies of the organization in which they are placed. Frequently only paid employees are covered.

In light of the number of schools without specific policies or with vague policies, the need is critical for specific and comprehensive policies to protect social work students in field placement and to inform social work supervisors and agency personnel of school policies.

Discussion

Sexual harassment in field instruction placements is likely to be a more pervasive problem than it is in the classroom or the laboratory. It is also more complicated to address and eliminate sexual harassment in practicum circumstances than in the more traditional and controlled components of the educational enterprise. This issue is of particular importance in social work education because of the extensive time devoted to field instruction in both BSW and MSW programs. It may be of equal importance, however, in medical internships, student teaching, nursing practica, and other human services educational enterprises.

It is clear to those who have examined sexual harassment issues in field instruction that interns are vulnerable in a variety of ways, some of which have been suggested in this study. The variety and complexity of these vulnerabilities are a result of the many roles represented in field placements. Although incidents between the field instructor or practicum supervisor and the student can usually be addressed because of the established relations between the program and the agency, other interactions may be more difficult to identify or address. For example, sexual harassment may be perpetrated within a field setting by staff members, who can range from executive-level personnel to maintenance people. Because students are often seen as those at the bottom of the organizational structure, staff at all levels may view them as targets for sexual harassment.

It is also possible that student-student sexual harassment may take place in field instruction settings. In some ways, such scenarios may be more difficult to address than those involving staff members and students. It is also possible for students to be the perpetrators of sexual harassment towards agency staff members and clients. While such improper behavior with clients may be addressed in a straightforward manner, the sexual harassment of staff by students raises more complex and subtle issues.

Purposes of Sexual Harassment Policies

Whatever the circumstances and whomever the actors, the basic purpose of any sexual harassment policy in field instruction is to protect everyone—agency personnel, students, and clients—from being victimized. For social work education programs, the primary purpose of such policies is to protect students. Therefore, the process of developing and implementing policies on sexual harassment should emphasize prevention rather than punishment or remediation. Effective policies will prevent students and others from experiencing the negative consequences of sexual harassment—consequences that may range from personal or psychological discomfort to inducement to leave the profession. Effective policies will also protect the integrity and quality of the profession. In the hostile environment that results from sexual harassment, the institutions suffer as well.

Developing Effective Policies

To develop effective policies, several important preconditions and guidelines, such as the following, should exist.

• Administrative support for a field placement sexual harassment policy is crucial if one is to be developed and taken seriously by faculty, students, and agency personnel. The chair, dean, or director of the program must be supportive of the policy and so must the person, persons, or committee responsible for administering the field instruction program. Involvement of the entire faculty in the development and implementation of the policies is crucial, especially in programs where faculty members serve in field liaison roles.

• An effective policy process should involve the students in its development and implementation. Students will be the primary source of reports of violations. Therefore, it is especially important for them to be involved in every phase of the process.

• Much can be accomplished through the involvement of field instruction personnel, such as agency executives and field instructors, in the development of the policy. They can be effective in guiding program personnel in the writing of policies and procedures that are applicable to the real situations of practice.

• It is worthwhile to obtain and use legal counsel in the development of sexual harassment policies. Each college or university's situation will be different. In some cases, the institutional sexual harassment policies cover students when they are involved in field instruction and no additional policies may be needed. In other cases, however, programs may need to develop their own policies. It is often useful to obtain the guidance of institutional legal counsel in the preparation of such policies.

• In many situations, a great deal can be achieved through the processes of consultation, negotiation, and education. It should be assumed that field instruction placements do not want sexual harassment to occur and are willing to take appropriate steps to prevent it. In many cases, agencies will already have their own policies or will be subject to government policies that apply to them. Sexual harassment may best be prevented by making agencies aware of the issue and securing their agreement to either enforce their own policies or abide by those promulgated by the educational program. Similarly, informing the field instructors themselves of the program's policies, either at training conferences or through liaison procedures, should help prevent incidents from occurring.

• Before beginning the process, policy developers should examine policies that are currently in effect. For example, the University of South Carolina's policy (see Appendix B) can be used as a model for other programs that wish to revise or strengthen their own sexual harassment policies.

Significant Findings

Perhaps the most significant finding of the research is that the assumed protection of students in field instruction does not, in reality, often exist. At a minimum, programs should determine the status of their sexual harassment policies and their applicability to the field instruction setting. Because field instruction in social agencies adds complexities to the whole issue, it is unwarranted to assume that the school's or university's internal policies are applicable without making a specific analysis.

Most important, perhaps, is the realization that procedures and policies on sexual harassment in the field setting are necessary components of a sound social work education program. Without them, all of the constituents—agency personnel, clients, field instructors, faculty, and, most important, students—may be victims of a hostile environment.

References

Adams, J. W., Kottke, J. L., & Padgitt, J. S. (1983). Sexual harassment of university students. *Journal of College of Student Personnel, 24*(6), 484-490.

Agencies no haven. (1984, April) *NASW News*, p. 5.

Blonston, G., & Scanlan, C. (1991, October 12). Hearing depicts war of sexes in workplace. *The State* [Columbia, SC], pp. 1A, 7A.

Brandenburg, J. B. (1982). Sexual harassment in the university: Guidelines for establishing a grievance procedure. *Signs, 8*(2), 320-336.

Brownmiller, G., & Alexander, D. (1992). From Carmita Wood to Anita Hill. *Ms., 2*(4), 70-71.

Cannon v. University of Chicago, 441 US 677, 60 LE 2d 560, 99 S. Ct. 1946. (1979).

Coles, F. S. (1986). Forced to quit: Sexual harassment complaint and agency response. *Sex Roles, 14*(1-2), 81-95.

Craib, R. (1977, July 22). Sex and women at UC Berkeley—Two surveys. *San Francisco Chronicle*.

Fitzgerald, L. F., Weitzman, L. M., Gold, Y., & Ormerod, M. (1988). Academic harassment: Sex and denial in scholarly garb. *Psychology of Women Quarterly, 12*, 329-340.

Hill, A. (1992). The nature of the beast. *Ms.*, *2*(4), 32-33.

Kaplan, S. J. (1991). Consequences of sexual harassment in the workplace. *Affilia, 6*(3), 50-65.

L. Robinson v. Jacksonville Shipyards, 760 F. Supp. 1486 (1991).

Livingston, J. A. (1982). Response to sexual harassment on the job: Legal, organizational and individual actions. *Journal of Social Issues, 38*(4), 5-22.

MacKinnon, C. (1979). *Sexual harassment of working women: A case of sex discrimination.* New Haven, CT: Yale University Press.

Meritor Savings Bank v. Vinson, 91 LE 2d 49, 106 S. Ct. 2399 (1986).

N. Jay Rogers v. EEOC, 454 F2d 234 (1972).

Perry, S. (1983, March 23). Sexual harassment on campus: Deciding when to draw the line. *Chronicle of Higher Education*, pp. 21-22.

Polakoff, S. E. (1984). A plan for coping with sexual harassment. *Journal of College Student Personnel, 25*(2), 165-167.

Pollack, W. (1990). Sexual harassment: Women's experience vs. legal definitions. *Harvard Women's Law Journal, 13*, 35-85.

Roscoe, B., Goodwin, M. P., Repp, S. E., & Rose, M. (1987). Sexual harassment of university students and student employees: Findings and implications. *College Student Journal, 21*(3), 254-273.

Schneider, B. E. (1987). Graduate women, sexual harassment, and university policy. *Journal of Higher Education, 58*(1), 46-65.

Scott, M. T. (1988). *Elements of sexual harassment.* Kent, OH: Kent State University.

Till, F. J. (1980). *Sexual harassment: A report on the sexual harassment of students.* Washington, DC: National Advisory Council on Women's Educational Programs.

Title VII of the 1964 Civil Rights Act, 42 U.S.C. Sec. 2000e-2000-17, 78 Stat. 255.

Title IX of the Education Amendments of 1972, 20 U.S.C. Sec. 1681-1686, 86 Stat. 373.

4

Human and Institutional Costs of Sexual Harassment

by Terry L. Singer

A 1989 survey of deans and directors of MSW programs (Singer, 1989) found that 54% of the responding programs had experienced incidents of sexual harassment over the previous five years. Most of these incidents involved the behavior of senior faculty members toward young women; about 25% of the reports concerned the behavior of practicum supervisors. The majority of deans/directors indicated that they followed up reports of abuse with direct contact with the parties involved. During informal discussions with this author, many deans and directors described their frustrations in handling the incidents—frustrations with lack of victim forthrightness due to fear of retaliation, frustrations with the responses of other faculty and students to the issues, and concerns about litigation, bad publicity, and pressures from higher university administrative offices to contain and resolve problems.

In a sense, these informal discussions with social work program administrators revealed their own feelings of vulnerability and, in some cases, victimization in the context of this problem. This chapter explores the cost of sexual harassment, not only to the direct victims of abuse, but also to institutions and persons associated with the phenomenon.

Although traditionally dismissed as harmless flirtation, sexual harassment is a serious abuse of power that occurs between two individuals who usually, but not always, possess unequal status in the workplace or the academic setting. Consequently, the individual who suffers the abuse may experience a number of adverse effects. The testimony of victims appearing in the media and a review of

Terry Singer is Dean of the School of Social Work, Marywood College.

current literature on sexual harassment point dramatically to the repercussions for the abused (Crull, 1982; Judd, Block, & Calkin, 1985; Kissman, 1990; Maypole, 1987). Job dissatisfaction, stress-related conditions, and mental health problems are some of the most common outcomes reported.

Several authors (Bergmann & Darity, 1981; Klein-Freada, 1984; Ledgerwood & Johnson-Dietz, 1981; Terpstra & Baker, 1986) identify the institutional and organizational costs of sexual harassment in their examination of negative impacts on productivity, liability, employee retention, and morale. The implication for employers (beyond the legal and moral issues) is that sexual harassment is bad business. One author (Garvey, 1986) details the costs of sexual harassment litigation to employers, citing examples of individual suits that resulted in large settlements, such as $15 million against ABC, $250,000 against CBS, and $150,000 against Union Pacific Railroad. According to Garvey, this kind of litigation may incur even higher costs, depending on the courts' extension of alternative theories of state tort actions. These might include assault and battery, intentional affliction of emotional distress, negligent infliction of emotional distress, intentional interference with contractual relations, negligence, gross negligence, or negligence in supervision and intrusion. The costs of litigation cited by Garvey (1986), as well as the costs associated with replacing those who quit their jobs because of harassment (identified by Terpstra and Baker, 1986), demonstrate that sexual harassment is a multi-million dollar concern of today's organizations. In fact, the United States Merit Systems Protection Board estimated that between May 1985 and May 1987 sexual harassment cost the federal government $267 million (Conte, 1990). The economic burdens imposed by sexual harassment are real and measurable, and employers must seek to reduce them, if only for the financial health of their organizations.

Although not necessarily separate from the economic variables of concern to management, other costs may also be attributed to sexual harassment. In this chapter, "costs" refers to human capital and the toll exacted from those who experience sexually harassing behavior in their workplace. As organizations have attempted to address the issue of sexual harassment, the personal costs to those associated with the experience have become increasingly evident. This chapter outlines the organizational and human costs in a system where a complaint has been filed.

The Abused

For those who are abused, the costs are well documented. In addition to experiencing the negative effects described previously, these victims may also suffer tribulations similar to those suffered by rape victims. Their character and sexual history may be put on trial in private and public hearings, particularly in formal hearings that involve legal representation. As with abused children who recount incidents of sexual abuse, victims of sexual harassment may not be believed. Additionally, in the most serious cases, these victims of harassment may share symptoms with those suffering from post-traumatic stress disorders. For example, in conversations with this author, many female victims reported recurring nightmares, nonspecific fears, and anger—years after the event. Others related incidents where good grades were promised in exchange for sex, and bold approaches were made to young women away from home for the first time. In one case, at the separate funerals of a student's mother and father, a faculty member in attendance attempted to proposition the student. The former student who related this incident was still terrified, years later, that the professor would reappear in her life someday.

Those who are victims of sexual harassment pay a dear price for their jobs or, in the case of those in school, for their degree. Many years after the fact, victims of abuse still hold memories of the experience, regardless of the final outcome.

Co-Workers

Co-workers are another group who share the costs of sexual harassment. In the case of a college, this group includes faculty and staff. Typically, these individuals are never apprised of the full facts of any abuse reported within the organization. They witness the trappings of the disciplinary process for the accused, but never with full understanding. The nature of the grievance process precludes any disclosure of information—at least by the management, academic officer, and other hearing officers. On the other hand, as is often the case, the accused is free to build a public case against the accuser, and may characterize the accuser's charges as discrimination, abuse of power, or willful misconduct. In numerous cases, civil suits initiated by either party may foster points of view or allegations that become part of the public record or press reports, and that ultimately become matters of discourse among co-workers.

Co-workers often feel betrayed when colleagues are charged with sexual harassment. In some cases, rumors of inappropriate behavior may portend such action, but often friendship blinds colleagues to such possibilities. Friendship and collegiality are challenged by information about sexual harassment charges, and often "camps" will materialize for and against both the accused and the accuser.

Management, which has the responsibility to weave through the complexities and charged atmosphere surrounding sexual harassment complaints, may become the focal point of varying public opinions. In an organization that depends upon cooperation, good will, and trust to facilitate its work, any tension or stress will have an impact on the system. Highly charged concerns such as sexual harassment may disrupt the balance sufficiently to distress the whole organization. In every sense of the metaphor, co-workers may behave as if they are part of a dysfunctional family. They too feel victimized.

Such feelings were reported by social work faculty members after a male colleague had been accused of sexual harassment. These faculty members, who felt forced to analyze their own behavior in this context, reported that they were questioning how well they handled gender-based issues. While the positive aspects of this questioning is evident, both male and female faculty members also discovered that a kind of defensiveness, cloaked in humor, had permeated school-wide relationships and created an atmosphere of tension. All felt held captive by the experience of this incident.

In the case of an educational institution, another group shares some of the characteristics of co-workers—students. They are also prone to feel frustrated by the lack of credible information and experience feelings of anger, betrayal, and tension. The same power differential between students and faculty that sets the stage for student victimization holds them at bay in the larger discussion. They may not readily enter into the public debate because they are still accountable in their coursework to faculty who have vested interests in the outcome of the complaint. Issues of classroom authority and objectivity may become skewed in such a heated academic arena. Students may feel forced by sociopolitical pressures to continue in the classroom as though there were no disturbances present.

Hearing Officers

Most organizations have a personnel committee (or some such group) to hear and process grievances and complaints. This may be composed of administrators, union representatives, or, in the case of AAUP colleges, faculty who have been elected to provide oversight. These committees generally operate under a seal of silence, are privy to the specifics of the charges, and often find themselves involved in clever legal machinations that delay and prolong the experience. In interviews with members of an administrative hearing committee, participants reported the extreme burden they felt in maintaining what they believed to be institutional "secrets." Efforts to be fair and just, to sort through the complexities of sexual harassment complaints, and to judge differing accounts of perceptions and reported abuses place such workers in very difficult positions. Some reported their concern about what their colleagues might be thinking of them. Their responsibility to maintain confidentiality regarding "the secret" is a cost that many who sit in judgment must bear alone. On the other hand, five years after presiding over a grievance hearing on sexual harassment by a colleague, a group of social work faculty related that a special bond had developed among those faculty who had "survived the ordeal."

The Accused

In a sense, those accused of sexual harassment are also victims. If they are innocent, the costs are obvious. Clouded by doubts that will persist and outlive any facts or findings, the accused innocent may have great difficulty in reclaiming their standing or credibility.

Those who are guilty of abuse, however, are also victims. Like rapists or child abusers, these perpetrators do not draw much sympathy or understanding for whatever psychosocial problems led them to these acts. With public disclosure, as limited in detail as it might be, they are often assumed to be guilty before the matter is even investigated.

The research on the extent of sexual harassment in schools of social work shows that many of the abusers are senior faculty. Linked to the power and authority of seniority, this dynamic of abuse is present in many institutions, businesses, and agencies; senior officials hold the power of office that enables them to inflict sexual harassment. Those who have risen through the ranks of professorship, tenure, and supervisory responsibilities—presumably through competence, mastery, and personal assuredness—often are reduced by charges of sexual harassment in the eyes of others. Through defensive postures of either attack or retreat, abusers frequently take on the appearance of a different person to prove their innocence to family, friends, colleagues, and the public. Many who have witnessed this phenomenon describe a form of pathos that evolves. At risk is a lifetime of professional development, current employment stability, and future ability to secure employment. Although abusers may be self-created victims, they must nevertheless pay great human costs and fight for their personal and professional lives.

Family Members

The families of those involved in incidents of sexual harassment—that is, the families of the victim, the abuser, and others who are close to the incident—are often overlooked when considering the human costs of this tragedy. Because sexual harassment involves a sad brutality of the human spirit, all who are exposed to it should find appropriate means to discuss the abuse. Their experience parallels that of overworked child welfare workers employed in crisis-ridden agencies who confront the stark realities of abuse with little supervision and support. In both circumstances, family members frequently become the recipients of unburdening psyches, and the scars of the involved individual become the scars of the family.

Nevertheless, little attention is given to those involved on the periphery. Those who experience the pain concomitant with allegations of sexual harassment may have a difficult burden to manage alone, and family support can minimize their alienation. This supportive role, however, places family members squarely within the fray. Thus, the families of those accused of sexual harassment are also victimized by the experience. They share in the public shame. In some cases, spouses, children, and other family members are ostracized by others in community and employment settings or become the focus of whispering campaigns. One public school report suggested that an abuser's child had regressed following the publication of news accounts regarding allegations against his father. The child was urinating in the classroom and demonstrating other signs of stress. Systematic examination of the experiences of family members surfaces the intricacies of relationships and how family members also feel victimized by the investigation process, revealing subsets of human interaction in which various victims emerge.

Executive Officer

For the purposes of this chapter, "executive officer" refers to the person who has major oversight responsibility for managing complaints in an organization. In many schools this is a dean or director. Even when organizations have complaint or grievance officers, the executive officer may hold responsibility for key decisions ranging from identifying the problem to resolving it. The executive officer is also privy to most of the information on the incident, whereas others, including the victim, are aware of only some of the information.

Although the filing of a sexual harassment complaint sets into motion a process that may have numerous twists and turns, there are commonalities among these processes. The executive officer will have to face many organizational dynamics, and must recognize that those involved will experience fear, surprise, and anger at the charges. These emotions, which are associated with accusation, will emanate from the victim, the accused, co-workers, and possibly others. During the process of resolution, emotions may change or intensify, and the resolution itself may generate yet another spate of emotions. These responses to the grievance process pose a great hurdle to the executive, who must endure and work with the emotions of self and of others.

The executive officer is often misunderstood because of the solitude of the position. Misinformation and direct personal attacks by vested interests will create additional burdens and challenges to this role. Conversations with deans and directors of schools and departments of social work have revealed that executive officers have been known to turn their backs to complaints, arrange deals with the accuser or accused, and even write positive recommendations to send their problems to other schools. The intention of revealing this is not to cast blame, but to acknowledge the stress placed on those who must respond to the problem and the inherent risk of victimization of the administrator.

A good executive officer will know how to recover some gains from the high institutional costs of a sexual harassment allegation. For example, the executive may initiate the development of new policies against harassment; new gender-sensitive material in institutional orientations, training sessions, and policy manuals; new organizational consciousness of the problem; and new avenues for justice for victims of sexual harassment.

Conclusion

It is a maxim of organizational theories that costs and benefits have to be analyzed carefully and understood to maintain the efficacy of any system. The literature has cataloged the monetary losses associated with sexual harassment incidents—litigation, lost work, and replacement training costs, to name a few. This author contends that the repercussions of sexual harassment are far greater than is generally assumed. In recognizing that the label of victim extends to so many, we must further recognize the potential impact on all those associated with organizations in which sexual harassment and/or sexual harassment accusations have occurred. This means that all organizations, including social work programs, should affirm a strong position against sexual harassment through mechanisms of education, research, policy directives, and standards. It is not only good business, it is also the right thing to do.

References

Bergmann, B. R., & Darity, W. (1981). Social relations, productivity, and employer discrimination. *Monthly Labor Review, 104(4),* 47-49.

Conte, A. (1990). *Sexual harassment in the workplace: Law and practice.* New York: John Wiley & Sons.

Crull, P. (1982). Stress effects of sexual harassment on the job: Implications for counseling. *American Journal of Orthopsychiatry, 52(3),* 539-544.

Garvey, M. S. (1986). The high costs of sexual harassment suits. *Personnel Journal, 65(1),* 75-78, 80.

Judd, P., Block, S. R., & Calkin, C. L. (1985). Sexual harassment among social workers in human service agencies. *Arete, 10(1),* 12-21.

Kissman, K. (1990). Women in blue-collar occupations: An exploration of constraints and facilitators. *Journal of Sociology and Social Welfare, 17(3),* 139-149.

Klein-Freada, R. (1984). *Sexual harassment in federal employment: Factors affecting its incidence, severity, duration, and relationship to productivity.* Unpublished doctoral dissertation, Brandeis University, MA.

Ledgerwood, D. E., & Johnson-Dietz, S. (1981). Sexual harassment: Implications for employer liability. *Monthly Labor Review, 104(4),* 45-47.

Maypole, D. E. (1987). Sexual harassment at work: A review of research and theory. *Affilia—Journal of Women and Social Work, 2(1),* 24-38.

Singer, T. L. (1989). Sexual harassment in graduate schools of social work: Provocative dilemmas. *Journal of Social Work Education, 25(1),* 68-76.

Terpstra, D. E., & Baker, D. D. (1986). Psychological and demographic correlates of perceptions of sexual harassment. *Genetic, Social, and General Psychology Monographs, 112(4),* 459-478.

5

The Role of Male Administrators in Preventing and Responding to Sexual Harassment

by Michael Reisch

T he strong and sustained reaction of many women and some men over the treatment of Professor Anita Hill by the all-male Judiciary Committee of the United States Senate in October 1991, and the political repercussions of this incident during the 1992 election campaign, underscore the seriousness with which sexual harassment issues are finally being addressed in U.S. society. More recently, widespread charges of sexual harassment in the armed forces during the Gulf War and during "routine" training exercises have led to major shakeups among military brass. Similar charges leveled against U.S. senators have already led to one senator's resignation and now threaten the careers of three more.

Although considerably less visible than such major societal institutions as the Pentagon and the Senate, schools of social work have not been immune from scandals involving allegations of sexual harassment. Recently, for example, accusations of sexual harassment brought by two undergraduate students at Humboldt State University against a faculty mentor led the California university to become the first in the state, and one of only a few in the country, to ban any sexual liaison between professors and students who are in their class or under their supervision. This incident of harassment, which received considerable media coverage, was unfortunately far from atypical. Studies cited by Singer in 1989 indicated that a majority of schools of social work had been confronted with cases of sexual harassment during the previous five years. Yet, in only 55% of these

Michael Reisch is Director of the Department of Social Work Education at San Francisco State University.

cases were incidents reported directly or indirectly to the school's dean or director. No data were collected on whether such matters were handled differently by male or female administrators. Since men still occupy a majority of the administrative positions in schools of social work, the ways that male administrators address an issue as serious as sexual harassment have implications not only for the individuals or the programs for which they have responsibility, but for the entire field.

In addressing the issue of sexual harassment, therefore, male administrators in schools of social work have to start with the premise that sexual harassment is not just a women's issue; it is a pervasive social problem that reflects historic patterns of societal oppression and discrimination that have had a particularly pernicious effect on women. In addition, sexual harassment affects the quality of collegial and faculty-student relationships in a school, and impacts upon faculty, students, and staff of both genders in a variety of areas that may not pertain directly to gender, sexuality, or power dynamics.

A Range of Inappropriate Responses

The tendency of most male administrators, however, is to treat the problem of sexual harassment along an inappropriate continuum ranging from nonresponsiveness to overreaction. Briefly, and unscientifically, these inappropriate responses can be characterized as follows:

• *The Boys-Will-Be-Boys Response.* This response regards the verbal or physical behavior of male harassers as a "normal" part of social interaction. In effect, this approach trivializes the impact of harassing behavior on its victims and, by interpreting the behavior as harmless flirtation, ignores the unequal individual and institutional power dynamics that underlie the relationship and allow the behavior to occur in the first place.

• *The Let's-Not-Get-Carried-Away-with-This Response.* This response recognizes that allegations of sexual harassment are a serious matter but would prefer for the incident to be handled at an informal level, either to avoid damage to the reputation of the accused and the school or to avoid the messy and time-consuming effort involved in pursuing such allegations through administrative channels. This response often occurs when the accused has no prior blemish on his record and when the school has no precedent for dealing with such matters. What such reactions ignore, however, are the organizational factors that may have prevented similar charges from surfacing before and the impact that brushing the matter aside—with whatever good intentions—may have on the subsequent climate of the school.

• *The We'll-Do-This-Strictly-by-the-Book Response.* While those who adopt this approach respond appropriately to sexual harassment allegations in administrative terms, they frequently fail to address with sensitivity the interpersonal and cultural consequences of such incidents on faculty, students, and staff. As a result, the *specific incident* may be handled correctly from a legal standpoint, but its wider and long-lasting repercussions will be ignored. Consequently, the feelings generated by the incident may fester and surface around other issues in which gender or power dynamics are a factor.

• *The My-God-This-Is-a-Crisis Response.* This response resembles a state of controlled panic. The administrator is so disturbed by the seriousness of the allegation and its short-term and long-term consequences that he sees the manifestations of the incident in all aspects of the school's life. In general, this is the approach adopted by a concerned individual who genuinely cares about those with whom he works but who has not taken any prior steps to address those factors in the organizational environment that might contribute to the emergence of sexual harassment cases. This response sometimes leads to misdirected concern and exaggerated reaction—sexual harassment is seen as a factor in all interpersonal problems within the school. Rather than mobilizing the school community in a positive direction, the effect of this response, particularly on those male faculty, staff, and students whose attention and support are most critical, is to promote avoidance of the subject, particularly in discussions between men and women.

Prevention Strategies

The recognition of sexual harassment as a form of social oppression requires male administrators to be aware of their own attitudes regarding oppression and sexism, as well as sexual harassment. The development of this awareness, however, requires more than introspection. Male administrators must listen carefully and openly to female colleagues, staff, and students and, in these interactions, adopt an open, learning, and self-critical posture, free of the defensiveness that so often surrounds such sensitive issues.

Although awareness and sensitivity are necessary, they are not sufficient conditions to arrest the onset of sexual harassment incidents. Male administrators must also create an environment that is receptive and sensitive to the discussion of the full range of women's concerns. This means that male administrators must listen to the needs and concerns of women on a broad range of issues. Women who feel uncomfortable speaking to their boss about salary and workload matters are certainly not going to to speak with him comfortably about sexual harassment.

Male administrators must then follow through in a timely fashion on the concerns raised in such discussions. By responding promptly, fully, and sensitively to issues generated by female staff and students, male administrators can create an atmosphere of trust in which sexual harassment cases can be presented openly. By developing an environment of mutual respect around a broad range of administrative problems, the insidious effects of a climate, characterized in an analogous context by Langston Hughes as "mutual strangeness," can be partially overcome.

Another step in this direction is to ensure that women's views on sexual harassment and other pertinent issues are heard—at all administrative levels—and via full, rather than token, participation in decision-making processes. A program in which women's perspectives are heard regularly on such issues as curriculum, faculty recruitment, and the distribution of assignments, and in which women are seen consistently and in significant numbers on decision-making bodies is more likely able to respond with sensitivity and effectiveness to sexual harassment issues.

Male administrators may also be viewed as role models for other males in the school in a range of capacities—as teacher, advisor, colleague, and mentor, as well as administrator. Given this potential status and influence, male administrators must avoid the appearance of encouraging or tolerating sexual harassment in any form—for example, silence or laughter in the presence of sexist humor or sexist discussions. A passive response to such situations can be interpreted as acceptance (if not approval) of such behavior and of the attitudes that underlie the behavior. The complicity, or at least insensitivity, that is implied by acquiescence in such circumstances undermines the ability of male administrators to take a forthright stand when more serious problems of sexual harassment come to their attention. To avoid any misinterpretation of their position on the issue of sexual harassment, male administrators must address offensive behavior firmly and directly as it occurs—that is, before a more serious problem develops or an environment conducive to or accepting of sexist behavior is established. However private collegial jokes or faculty discussions might seem, the campus grapevine may transmit male administrators' responses or nonresponses throughout the school community.

Serving as a positive role model is but one of the educational functions that male administrators should serve in handling the issue of sexual harassment with faculty, staff, and students. Another function should be to open up a continuing dialogue about the nature of sexual harassment and its linkages to sexism and other forms of individual and societal oppression. This dialogue should include discussion on the important difference between sexual behavior—in which all people engage (albeit with cultural and gender differences)—and sexual harassment—which exploits the lopsided power dynamics of an interpersonal relationship. It is equally important to identify sexual harassment as unethical behavior that is intolerable from anyone aspiring to be a social worker or social work educator.

In the process of educating faculty, staff, and students, male administrators must also show sensitivity to the connections between sexual harassment, racism, and homophobia. This is particularly crucial in programs that have diverse student and faculty populations, because tensions around racial and ethnic differences often complicate the prevention and resolution of sexual harassment incidents. Male administrators should create opportunities for these issues to be discussed prior to the onset of a problem. In relation to these discussions, however, male administrators must be careful to avoid fostering a "hierarchy of oppression," in which diverse populations compete for protected status or, worse, for designation as the "most victimized" or "most discriminated against."

Response Strategies

Even under the best of circumstances, sexual harassment allegations may arise. Male administrators are under a particularly strong imperative to respond fully and promptly to all such allegations from whatever source. They must not allow concerns for protecting the alleged perpetrator or, for that matter, the image of the program to prevent a full and fair inquiry into the matter. In fact, the program's reputation is likely to be enhanced by a thorough and effective investigation. Administrators may be able to safeguard the reputations of both the school and the accused by attempting to resolve the issue at the school level and by maintaining strict confidentiality once the investigation of a sexual harassment complaint begins.

Once the inquiry is initiated, it is also important to make sure that all parties to the alleged incident—including the school community—understand the processes to be followed. Ongoing education about the rights and responsibilities of all members of the school community—including confidentiality and freedom from reprisal—can facilitate this understanding.

In addition to educating the community about the investigative process, male administrators should demonstrate their commitment to the process of investigating, decision making, and sanctioning. This commitment will help ensure that justice is obtained and that the confidence of the school community is not diminished. Often, such cases have bizarre twists and turns. Male administrators should be prepared to stay with the process through direct, close, and ongoing involvement; this focus is critical to protecting the rights of all parties concerned and to maintaining administrative credibility if future controversies arise, as they inevitably will.

Although the specifics of any investigation must be kept confidential, the approach to ultimate handling of the incident are likely to become widely known. Both the process and the results of the investigation will influence future relationships within the school and will affect the administrator's capacity to deal with colleagues and students on other sensitive issues. Therefore, male administrators must be prepared to deal with the aftermath of such cases within the school, university, and professional communities. In part, this may be done by ensuring that whatever sanctions are imposed are significant and understood in terms of the seriousness of the act. In other words, male administrators should not allow the act of punishing the perpetrator to shift the sympathies of the communities in his/her favor. Instead, male administrators should use the incident to educate, with the future well-being of the school always in mind.

Conclusion

Given the long history of social inequality in our society and the recent upsurge in misogynistic cultural patterns, it is unlikely that administrators in any school of social work, even under the best of circumstances, will be able to completely prevent incidents of sexual harassment. Instead, they should establish guidelines for proactive, preventative approaches to the issue and for fair, sensitive, and effective processes for handling incidents. Briefly, the guidelines presented here emphasized the following points for male administrators.

- They should recognize and find ways to assert that sexual harassment is related to power dynamics and social inequality, not sexuality. Making connections between sexual harassment and other forms of institutional and individual oppression is an important component of the process of sensitizing faculty, staff, and students to the proper definition of the issue.
- They should establish open and ongoing dialogues with female faculty, staff, and students on a wide range of issues. In this regard, they should adopt the role of learner and be willing to engage in reflection on and self-criticism of their own behaviors.
- They should take proactive steps to create a harassment-free work and educational environment, in part by serving as a role model for faculty and students.
- When incidents occur, administrators should be focused, consistent, and sensitive to all those affected. They should recognize the long-term implications of how they respond to allegations of sexual harassment and the educational opportunities presented during the allegation, investigation, and sanctioning process.

Although these guidelines are intended to apply to all administrators, they are viewed as particularly important in helping male administrators to confront their own attitudes and actions regarding sexual harassment. The level of mistrust between men and women is higher today than it has been for many decades. In part, this is due to the recent increase in anti-female attitudes in our culture and public policies, and to the resurgence of feminism in response. In part, however, the mistrust reflects the changing patterns of gender relations in our society which, in turn, are part of a broader societal upheaval. Although the general direction of gender relations may be toward greater equality, the persistence of sexual harassment indicates how far we still have to go. As a profession long dedicated to principles of social justice and human dignity, social work should certainly be a leader in the development of learning environments in which these principles are put into practice.

Sources Consulted

Annotated bibliography on sexual harassment in education. (1982). *Women's Rights Law Reporter, 7*(2).

Benson, D. J., & Thomson, G. E. (1982). Sexual harassment on a university campus: The confluence of authority relations, sexual interest and gender stratification. *Social Problems, 29,* 236-252.

Carroll, L., & Ellis, K. L. (1989). Faculty attitudes towards sexual harassment: Survey results, survey process. *Journal of the National Association for Women Deans, Administrators and Counselors, 52*(3), 35-42.

Crocker, P. L. (1983). An analysis of university definitions of sexual harassment. *Signs, 8,* 696-707.

Dziech, B. W., & Weiner, L. (1984). *The lecherous professor: Sexual harassment on campus.* Boston: Beacon Press.

Faludi, S. (1991). *Backlash: The undeclared war against American women.* New York: Crown Publishers.

Fitzgerald, L. F. (1988). Academic harassment: Sex and denial in scholarly garb. *Psychology of Women Quarterly, 12,* 329-340.

Hoffman, F. L. (1986). Sexual harassment in academia: Feminist theory and institutional practice. *Harvard Educational Review, 56*(2), 105-121.

Keller, E. (1990, January/February). Consensual relationships and institutional policy. *Academe,* 29-32.

Kenig, S., & Ryan, J. (1986). Sex differences in levels of tolerance and attribution of blame for sexual harassment on a university campus. *Sex Roles, 15,* 433-442.

Maypole, D. E. (1986). Sexual harassment of social workers at work: Injustice within? *Social Work, 31* (1), 29-34.

Olson, C., & McKinney, K. (1989). Processes inhibiting the reduction of sexual harassment in academe: Alternative explanation. *Journal of the National Association for Women Deans, Administrators and Counselors, 52*(3), 7-14.

Paludi, M. A. (1991). *Ivory power: Sexual harassment on campus.* New York: State University of New York Press.

Reilly, M. E., Lott, B., & Gallogly, S. M. (1986). Sexual harassment of university students. *Sex Roles, 15,* 333-358.

Robertson, C., Dyer, C. E., & Campbell, D. (1988), Campus harassment: Sexual harassment policies and procedures at institutions of higher learning. *Signs, 13*(4), 792-812.

Schneider, B. E. (1987). Graduate women, sexual harassment and university policy. *The Journal of Higher Education, 58*(1), 46-65.

Singer, T. (1989). Sexual harassment in graduate schools of social work: Provocative dilemmas. *Journal of Social Work Education, 25* (1), 68-76.

Stimpson, C. R. (1989). Over-reaching: Sexual harassment. *Journal of the National Association for Women Deans, Administrators and Counselors, 52* (3), 1-6.

Sullivan, M., and Bybee, D. I. (1987, Winter). Female students and sexual harassment. What factors predict reporting behavior? *Journal of the National Association for Women Deans, Administrators and Counselors,* 11-16.

Terpstra, D. E., and Baker, D. D. (1987). A hierarchy of sexual harassment. *Journal of Psychology, 121,* 599-607.

6

Planning for Prevention of Sexual Harassment at the University of Washington's School of Social Work

by Nancy R. Hooyman and Lorraine Gutiérrez

T his chapter provides an overview of planning and policy initiatives at the University of Washington's School of Social Work
to prevent sexual harassment. It highlights the development of
policies and procedures recommended by a task force composed of
faculty, students, and staff, and concludes with recommendations for
comparable planning initiatives. This participatory, educational,
open approach to creating a safe environment was consistent with
ongoing efforts to implement feminist values within the organization. By promoting discussion and education, encouraging problem-
solving behavior, and creating a supportive environment, the School
provided all members of its community with opportunities to be
involved in preventing harassment.

Background

The impetus for this planning and policy initiative was a series of
sexual harassment complaints filed by students against faculty members over a six-month period. The primary step for attempting to
resolve such complaints is the University's Ombudsman for Sexual
Harassment, who handles about 40 to 50 complaints of sexual
harassment a year from across the campus. The ombudsman is able

*Nancy Hooyman is Dean and Professor of Social Work, University of Washington.
Lorraine Gutiérrez is Associate Professor of Social Work, University of Washington.*

Special appreciation and acknowledgment are extended to members of the Task
Force for the Prevention of Sexual Harassment: Reiko Hayashi, Nanci Nelson,
Nikki Nicotera, Cindy Riche, and Emily Salois.

to resolve over 90% of the complaints in her office without moving to a formal procedure. She pursues an educational and mediational approach in which both the individuals involved are asked to provide descriptions of what occurred, to put their experiences in writing, and then to meet with her and the appropriate administrative head to attempt to reach an agreement about what occurred and how the situation can be satisfactorily resolved.

In all instances that have involved social work students and faculty, complaints have been satisfactorily resolved by the informal mechanism: The harassers recognized the inappropriateness of what had occurred, apologized for their actions, and agreed upon procedures by which they would relate to the victims in the future. The victims expressed their satisfaction at being heard and their feelings of being empowered by the process.

Although these complaints were successfully resolved, a sense of unease lingered among the students. As they learned about sexual harassment incidents from other students, many became anxious about their own safety. Part of the schoolwide effort to implement feminist values has been to create open and two-way channels of communication between social work faculty and students. Therefore, it was important to bring allegations and resolutions into the open for systematic discussion among faculty, staff, and students (assuming the permission of the individuals involved) rather than having them remain at the level of hallway talk. The goal was to create an overall positive and comprehensive approach toward learning about, preventing, and eliminating harassment, rather than remaining focused on a few specific instances. In doing so, we hoped to avoid fostering a solely reactive and punitive stance.

Two Parallel Initiatives

The first initiatives took place on two parallel levels: among the students themselves and among the School's elected Executive Committee, which is the primary faculty governance mechanism. Forming a Coalition against Sexual and Malicious Harassment, the students circulated a letter to their peers, stating their overall aim to create a supportive and safe environment for students. This letter reviewed the incidents of harassment that had occurred in the preceding six months and publicized that a group of students were willing to provide advocacy and support for anyone who had been affected by harassment at any point during their association with the School. They also created anti-harassment buttons that were distributed at graduation. One positive aspect of this student-led campaign was the degree of visibility it gave to the problem. By bringing these issues into the open, this student group provided further impetus to create a more systematic organizational response.

Unfortunately, this campaign had negative consequences as well. Because this letter recounted the earlier incidents of harassment, it had the unfortunate effect of increasing anxiety among some students. Another limitation was that it was directed only to students, thereby failing to involve faculty and staff in an educational and supportive approach. Thus, the campaign ran counter to the goal of trying to involve all members of the School community in positive educational initiatives.

The Faculty Executive Committee approached the problem with the goal of creating and sustaining a nondiscriminatory and mutually supportive workplace through education and prevention, rather than reacting to specific problems or incidents. Their focus was to encourage faculty dialogue and problem solving around the complex issues related to harassment. Underlying the Executive Committee's action was the faculty's own uncertainty and unease about how to handle classroom and social situations in what had become an increasingly emotionally charged atmosphere, given the students' focus on the past incidents. In fact, some faculty felt that "students were out to get them" while others became informal confidantes and advisers to the student group—a dynamic that had the potential to divide the faculty.

The Executive Committee recognized that the School's increasingly diverse student body was complicating the matter: faculty who were accustomed to fairly homogeneous student groups were dealing with many changes. The tensions related to sexual harassment were interconnected with and often exacerbated by ethnic, racial, generational, and religious differences between students and faculty. Recognizing the tensions created by the larger contextual changes, the Executive Committee was concerned that faculty have opportunities to seek solutions to these issues before moving to any collaborative educational efforts with students.

In an effort to create these opportunities, three highly respected senior faculty circulated a memo asking faculty to share related incidents from both classroom and social situations for which they would welcome consultation and advice regarding appropriate behavior. A small number of faculty responded with a list that included classroom simulations and exercises involving behavior that could be perceived as harassing (such as hugging someone), faculty interactions with students in School social events, and junior/senior faculty mentoring relationships, which warranted particular analysis since most of the junior faculty were women and most of the senior faculty were men. Some faculty expressed a genuine sense of regret about their declining participation in School-sponsored social gatherings due to their fear of entering a situation that could be experienced as harassing by students. Others expressed regrets that they had little contact with junior faculty, fearing that a mentoring situation intended to be helpful, such as meeting for coffee or drinks to talk about research, could be interpreted as harassing. Although they clearly recognized the inappropriateness of sexual harassment under any conditions, faculty also acknowledged their uncertainty about appropriate boundaries for classroom, mentoring, and social interactions.

The Task Force

Although both the student and faculty initiatives were successful in heightening awareness of and educating others about sexual harassment and the resources available to handle and prevent it, there was concern that these planning efforts did not involve staff and were not interconnected, thus running contrary to administrative priorities on inclusiveness. No mechanism existed for faculty, staff, and students to meet together to talk openly about sexual harassment. In an effort to build a sense of community around shared goals of prevention and safety, a Task Force of faculty, staff, and students, chaired by a staff member, was appointed by the Dean and charged with developing recommendations for the entire School community. The Task Force was composed of an assistant professor, students representing all three degree programs, and one staff person. All were women, three were people of color, and several were lesbians. In creating the committee, an effort was made to well represent groups that are particularly vulnerable to sexual and other types harassment and that have a strong commitment to preventing harassing behavior.

The remainder of this chapter documents the implementation of these recommendations, which broaden the scope of prevention beyond sexual harassment itself to other types of insensitive, harassing, and discriminatory behavior. Early in the process, the Task Force recognized the interconnections among sexual harassment, sexism, racism, homophobia, and other forms of individual and societal oppression—that is, all spring from relationships characterized by power inequities, and all negatively affect the learning and work environment.

The activities recommended by the Task Force were focused on achieving the following three goals:

- To educate students, faculty, and staff about harassment and the resources available within the School and the University for handling instances of harassment and discrimination.
- To empower students and staff by teaching and modeling constructive responses to insensitive, harassing, or discriminatory incidents.
- To enhance faculty skills in teaching and relating to an increasingly diverse student population.

Education of Faculty, Students, and Staff

A range of activities, recommended by the Task Force and readily implemented, was intended to make procedures and resources visible and accessible to the entire School community. As students had defined in the written materials distributed through their Coalition Against Harassment, the underlying objective of all these activities was to make the School a "harassment-free zone" for all its members. One of the first tasks was to develop symbolic representations of this objective.

Brightly colored posters with educational messages were developed and placed around the building. The posters were intended to create an organizational atmosphere in which harassment of any kind is not tolerated. One set of posters described specific incidents or "trigger events" to charges of sexual harassment, all of which had occurred in the School but which were portrayed anonymously to assure confidentiality. Presenting a brief description of an incident, each poster asks the question: "Is this harassment?" Steps that could be taken if someone experienced such a situation were then clearly identified. (See Figure 1.)

The posters were intended to serve as foci for motivating thought and discussion about perceptions of harassment. Encouraging such discussion was viewed as central to creating an overall safe and positive learning environment. (Examples of other posters are presented in Appendix C.)

Another poster presented a flow chart of steps to take if one felt harassed within the School because of race, gender, religion, ethnic background, disability, or sexual orientation. It outlined the individuals and offices that students, faculty, or staff could access to talk to someone about a harassing incident. The procedures were differentiated in terms of an informal complaint procedure within the

Figure 1. Poster distributed in the University of Washington's School of Social Work

---

Is This Harassment?

> A first-year MSW student has a practicum in which she is working with individuals and families. She really loves the work, but has noticed that her practicum supervisor often begins their meetings by commenting on her appearance or the physical attractiveness of her female clients. When she mentions that this makes her uncomfortable, he tells her not to be so sensitive.

Harassment is behavior that intimidates or demeans others. It can be verbal, written, or physical. If you experience harassment in the School of Social Work or in a practicum agency, tell someone by calling the University or the School of Social Work Ombudsman, or by talking with a faculty member.

Talking about harassment is one way to stop it
and prevent its reoccurrence!

School of Social Work, an informal complaint procedure within the University of Washington, a formal complaint procedure within the University, and an action outside the University's jurisdiction.

Another poster, *Six Things I've Always Wanted to Know about Harassment . . . but was Afraid to Ask*, used a question-and-answer format to portray the myths and facts about harassment. (See Appendix C.) This poster was particularly useful for answering common questions about harassment in a straightforward manner.

The Task Force also developed a pamphlet on peer harassment. Although they recognized that most instances of harassment involved misuse of power toward someone in a subordinate position, they were aware of situations where peers had acted in harassing, intimidating, or demeaning ways to other students on the basis of their race, religion, age, marital status, physical disability, sexual orientation, gender, or identification with a particular group. The peer harassment brochure was not only publicized through posters but placed in the mail file of every student, faculty, and staff person. (See Appendix C.)

In an effort to convey institutional support for creating and sustaining a safe community, the Dean wrote a letter in which the School was characterized as an academic community dedicated to the ideals of social justice in theory and in daily practice, and in which procedures were outlined within the School and the University for preventing and eliminating discriminatory and harassing behavior. The tone of the letter conveyed that incidents involving harassment and discrimination are considered unethical and will not be tolerated under any conditions; that such incidents are taken very seriously and that addressing them is the highest priority; that complainant confidentiality is assured; that options for action exist; and that the complainant remains "in the driver's seat" about how many and which steps to take before using formal procedures. This letter was placed on large posters in key locations around the building, mailed to all entering students, included in the student handbook, and distributed at orientation and to the mail files of all faculty, staff, and students. Copies of this letter were also published in the School's internal newsletter, as well as partially reproduced in the School's external newsletter that is mailed to all alumni, practicum instructors, and Visiting Committee members.

A comprehensive "Anti-Harassment Resources Notebook" was compiled, including the University's official *Stop Sexual Harassment* pamphlet, page-size copies of the posters, the Washington State Criminal Code regarding harassment, the Women's Rights Complaints Procedures, the Human Rights Complaints Procedures, and a Peer Harassment pamphlet. This Notebook is available in the reserve section of the School of Social Work library. In addition, the University Ombudsman, the School of Social Work Ombudsman, and a representative of the Task Force speak at orientation for new students in the fall, and the University Ombudsman is available to provide additional training to students, staff, and faculty. In fact, the University *requires* that faculty and staff participate in harassment training, offered by the University Ombudsman, every two years.

The posters, letters, "Anti-Harassment Resources Notebook," and regularly scheduled training on sexual harassment convey information in highly visible and accessible ways. These materials and the dissemination of policies illustrating the stance held by the institution and by the Dean serve to educate the School community about harassment of all types.

Empowerment and Learning/Teaching in a Diverse Community

A by-product of the focus on sexual harassment training was an effort to increase community sensitivity about all types of harassing behaviors. Two initiatives—a panel on sensitivity and diversity training—had the following objectives:

- To increase the level of sensitivity about harassing and discriminatory behavior.
- To help students, faculty, and staff work effectively in a diverse community.
- To inform students, faculty, and staff about what to do when encountering insensitive behavior.

The panel of faculty, staff, and students, which included individuals of color, gay men, and lesbian women, was intended to heighten awareness about personal experiences with harassing and discriminatory behavior. This panel, which was scheduled at a time that would not conflict with classes, was widely publicized to faculty, students, staff, and practicum instructors. Panelists talked openly and poignantly about their experiences with harassing or discriminatory behavior in the School or the larger University community. Listening to others talk about their feelings and experiences was an extremely powerful educational tool for both the participants and the audience. Key to the panel's success was participants' willingness to adopt a nonjudgmental tone in discussing their experiences. The audience, in turn, was encouraged to ask questions and to share their reactions in as nondefensive a manner as possible. Members of the audience reported that these personal stories had a more profound effect on them than had any prior educational formats where information was simply transmitted. Given the success of this program, similar annual panels were planned.

Diversity training was also offered to all faculty, staff, and students as part of the School's commitment to practice social justice and to celebrate the richness and strengths of diversity. This training, which has an educational and preventive focus, does not cover harassment per se but rather learning and working effectively with those who are different from ourselves. By working to create an atmosphere in which diversity is truly valued, we hope not only to develop an environment in which harassment is viewed and treated as an intolerable act, but to eradicate it from our community. Valuing diversity means moving beyond forbearance or acceptance to understanding and support of people of different colors, cultures, abilities, gender, and orientation. The training is based on the premise that we all have more to learn about how to listen and work with those who differ from us; and that the process of valuing diversity begins with understanding our own fears and biases.

Follow-up to diversity training is particularly important. After the workshops, a group of faculty continued to meet monthly to discuss issues related to teaching in diverse classrooms, and a group of staff, which cross-cut different levels and units in the School, began plans to implement specific recommendations that emerged from the staff diversity training. One recommendation that reached fruition was a combined faculty/staff retreat at the beginning of the year. (In the past, faculty and staff retreats had been held separately.) This event provided opportunities for faculty and staff to begin to get to know each other in an informal setting outside the hierarchical relationships of the work environment. Ongoing sustained efforts, however, are needed to create a work environment where staff members feel that their contributions to the School are valued and fully recognized by faculty. Diversity training for students is voluntary, offered in the evenings and weekends, and complements a foundation course in Societal Oppression and Diversity that they must take in their first quarter.

A caveat for those implementing diversity training, however, is to assure that the value placed on diversity does not give license to use words or actions that, although they may be acceptable in some cultures, could limit, offend, or hurt people in other cultures. At times, there may be an inherent tension between respecting differences and preventing/eliminating sexual harassment. It is important that trainers provide opportunities for open discussion regarding these complex issues.

Factors Conducive to Creating a Safe Learning Environment

Although these recent efforts at the University of Washington's School of Social Work continue to evolve and to be evaluated, a number of key factors have emerged for planning policies and programs to prevent harassing and discriminatory behavior.

- *Gaining support and resources from the top.* Both the University as a whole, through the resources provided to the Office of the Ombudsman for Sexual Harassment and the Human Rights Office, and the School of Social Work administrative offices have made strong, visible statements that sexual harassment will not be tolerated under any circumstances. This is evidenced not only through written and verbal announcements, but also by behavior that conveys the seriousness of harassing incidents. Complaints are acted upon immediately, sending the message to students, faculty, and staff about the priority placed upon their resolution by the administration.

- *Making policies and procedures highly visible.* Both the University and the School's policies toward creating safe and supportive environments are highly visible to faculty, staff, and students. Information is presented to students from their admission to the School until their graduation. The first packet of material sent to entering students includes the policies and procedures related to sexual harassment as well as the Dean's letter conveying our commitment to a harassment-free community. New faculty, including practicum instructors and staff, also receive copies of these policies. The Dean has periodically written about sexual harassment for the School's internal newsletter. As noted before, posters about harassment and relevant procedures/polices are placed around the building.

- *Developing a coalition of faculty, staff, and students.* As noted, our initial efforts were not coordinated or comprehensive, and they excluded staff, thereby failing to develop shared objectives for the entire School community. As a result of the appointment of a Task Force composed of faculty, staff, and students, common concerns and goals were identified. The collaborative approach has carried over into other activities, such as planning for the fall faculty and staff retreat, and will be used in developing other anti-harassment activities.

- *Expanding the focus to include harassing and discriminatory behavior of any kind.* Given the increasingly diverse student, staff, and faculty bodies in our School, it was important to recognize the seriousness of all types of harassing and discriminatory behavior, and to disabuse our community of the notion that sexual harassment is primarily a male faculty-female student issue. The activities and collaborative planning we carried out provided a sense of collective responsibility among all members of the School to create a safe environment for all persons and helped us to recognize that behaviors and attitudes learned in working with diverse populations will ultimately serve to prevent sexually harassing behavior. The danger of this approach, however, is that by broadening the focus, the pervasive and insidious nature of sexual harassment and the inherent gender and power inequities will be downplayed. Ongoing training by the Ombudsman for Sexual Harassment, publication of the University's and School's policies regarding sexual harassment, and continued discussions of issues raised by sexual harassment are essential to counter any such tendency.

- *Institutionalizing of activities.* We found it important to build in mechanisms and resources to support the continuation of the Task Force recommendations, including the panel on sensitivity and the diversity training. While recognizing the changing needs of faculty, staff, and students, we wanted to establish routines and expectations for behavior at the School. It is also important, however, to evaluate the efficacy and desirability of each initiative over time. For example, the posters should be periodically reviewed and updated to make sure that information is accurate and timely; diversity training should be modified to take into account those who have already participated in similar training and who have different levels of knowledge and awareness of the issue; and the sensitivity panel should be changed to match participants' experiences.

Challenges

Despite institutionalization of these activities, future budget cutbacks could challenge our ability to support them at an adequate funding level and to provide them annually. In addition, given the central role of the practicum experience to the students' education, the School should extend such annual training and education to the practicum. Ongoing research should also be conducted, both to document the incidence of sexual harassment and to determine whether educational and preventive approaches have any impact over time. Anecdotal information from students, who state that the posters, letters, and training have made the School seem welcoming and safe to them, suggest the effectiveness of this approach, and no complaints about harassment have been raised since the implementation of the Task Force recommendations, but these efforts must still be systematically evaluated.

Last, we must not become complacent. Although the School can be proud of its plans and policies to create a safe and supportive environment, we are all prone to slipping back into old modes of behavior and attitudes. Living with diversity and with changing norms and rules about appropriate behaviors can be painful as we confront uncertainties, contradictions, and conflicts that arise from changes in traditional boundaries and world views. Accordingly, all members of the School community need to be a part of regularly recurring educational and prevention efforts; no training is "too simple" or "too basic," and no one should be excused from such initiatives because they maintain that they don't need it. An important message to be conveyed is that we always have more to learn about others and ourselves, especially in increasingly diverse environments.

7

Creating a Positive Environment for Learning and Working

by Marie O. Weil, Nancy R. Hooyman, and Michelle Hughes

> In matters of race and gender, it is now possible and necessary, as it seemed never to have been before, to speak about these matters without the barriers, the silences, the embarrassing gaps in discourse.
>
> —*Toni Morrison (1992)*

As we have seen in the preceding chapters, the issue of sexual harassment challenges us as social work educators and practitioners. Sexual, gender, and power issues, which lie at the core of harassment and can arouse intense feelings of discomfort and anger, heighten the complexity of the problem. An additional complicating factor is the interconnection among sexual harassment, sexism, racism, homophobia, and other forms of individual and societal oppression. Given this complexity, it is not surprising that many of us are struggling to find ways to deal positively and proactively with sexual harassment. The search for new models of behavior is not easy. For all of us, it is to some degree a struggle to learn new, nonexploitative ways to relate to those who are different from us, for we have all been socialized within oppressive systems.

Reactions to Increased Awareness of Sexual Harassment

Larger societal changes set the context within which we learn to deal with issues of sexual harassment. As a result of demographic changes, increased mobility, escalating economic pressures, and

Marie Weil is Professor of Social Work, University of North Carolina, Chapel Hill. Nancy Hooyman is Dean and Professor of Social Work, University of Washington. Michelle Hughes is an MSW student, University of North Carolina, Chapel Hill.

changing definitions of sex roles and responsibilities, men and women are challenged to define new ways of interacting with one another. Yet these changes, particularly as women move into positions of power previously denied to them, can create economic and psychological insecurity for those who are accustomed to maintaining power. These tensions can be exacerbated when issues that touch at the core of interpersonal relationships are raised by charges of sexual harassment.

When women, who have traditionally been denied power and equal status, assert that they will no longer tolerate harassing behavior, norms that have governed past behavior are challenged dramatically. These challenges, and concomitant calls for change, can cause several types of reactions among those who have traditionally held power. These reactions, identified in the earlier chapters, represent a continuum ranging from: (1) strong agreement with the need for policies, as well as relief about and approval of their implementation; (2) neutrality; (3) an uneasiness and heightened sensitivity about how to relate to others, manifested by concern over appropriate boundaries and behavior; (4) defensiveness and hostility about the issue of sexual harassment and toward anyone who raises the issue, or what Michael Reisch terms the "let's-not-get-carried-away-with-this" response; and (5) hostile backlash against the recognition of and movement against sexual harassment, manifested by claims that policies prohibiting harassing behavior infringe on an individual's civil or academic rights.

Positive Reactions

For many, the development and implementation of policies are seen as long overdue. For almost a decade, research reports have revealed that a significant number of female students in universities and colleges experience some form of harassing behavior (Robertson, Dyer, & Campbell, 1985; Roscoe, Goodwin, Repp, & Rose, 1987; Schneider, 1987). Female faculty have also reported sexual harassment as a serious problem. A 1986 study conducted at Harvard by the Association of American Colleges revealed that 32% of tenured women faculty and 49% of untenured women faculty reported that they were subjected to job-related sexual harassment (as cited in Kantrowitz, 1992, p. 21). Thus, it is no surprise that a majority of women faculty and students, as well as many of their male colleagues, have expressed relief and approval of new policies prohibiting sexual harassment in academic settings. They perceive the implementation of these policies as a vital step in the creation of a safe and supportive learning environment for all members of the academic community.

Neutral Reactions

Other individuals may not see the need for such policies, but on the other hand, do not oppose them. They may demonstrate a neutral stance toward sexual harassment policies because they do not perceive sexual harassment as an issue that concerns or affects them. These individuals may be men who do not perceive themselves as harassers, or women who feel that they can handle any situation that comes their way.

Heightened Sensitivity

A third reaction, heightened sensitivity and uneasiness toward the issues of sexual harassment, may manifest itself in a variety of ways. Faculty may refuse to attend social events for fear of being accused of acting inappropriately. They may stop meeting with students in their offices, insisting that they meet in a location where behavior can be observed and not later misconstrued; or they may insist on keeping their office doors open when they meet with students, thereby inhibiting private conversation. Others may refuse to use role plays or simulations in classes for fear that behavior that could be viewed as harassing may occur within the context of the exercise. Senior faculty members (often men) may feel uncomfortable meeting with junior faculty (usually women) for coffee or drinks, and may act extremely guarded with them. Such uneasiness and concern over appropriate boundaries should not be viewed solely in a negative light. It is a natural consequence of examining personal behavior toward and attitudes about others in response to a changing sociopolitical context. Prolonged uneasiness and guarded behavior, however, may indicate an inability to understand and accept the positive aspects of challenging and changing the status quo in regard to this issue.

Strong Negative Reactions

Stronger negative responses to sexual harassment include minimizing or trivializing the existence and impact of harassment, making jokes about harassment to discredit initiatives to address it, denying the existence of the problem, and blaming women for harassing behavior (Faludi, 1993). We have all heard comments such as "It was just harmless flirtation," "You can't even tell a women she looks nice anymore without being sued," "Women should be flattered by that kind of attention," and "She approached him first." Such reactions deny the reality of sexual harassment as a form of social oppression and seek to discredit the damaging impact that sexual harassment has upon the lives of individuals and the entire academic community.

One Type of Backlash Reaction

Finally, as the issues of sexual harassment have become increasingly publicized and victims more vocal about their experiences, there are some who have taken reactionary stances against efforts to establish sexual harassment as a significant and destructive force. Two types of backlash have emerged. The first often manifests itself as an argument that current policies against sexual harassment violate or infringe upon civil or academic rights. For example, it has been argued that the legal definition of sexual harassment has been expanded too broadly in the area of "hostile environment" (Cohen, 1992). Other public arguments have held that current definitions of and policies against sexual harassment threaten or discriminate against men (Leo, 1992; Weiss, 1992). Finally, some have asserted that efforts to acknowledge the damaging impact of sexually or racially offensive comments and prevent their occurrence violate the right to freedom of speech. These arguments may also characterize such efforts as overzealous attempts to mandate "politically correct speech."

This set of reactions has escalated into a concerted attempt to undermine activities and concerns related to sexual harassment. Those that favor this stance view the development and implementation of clear, strong policies and procedures prohibiting sexually harassing behavior as indicative of a punitive approach that seeks to restrict academic and individual freedom (Davidson, 1992). Evidence of this view is seen in recent media coverage that has documented backlash against university policies seeking to prevent racial, sexual, and sexual orientation harassment. Some have attacked the right or ability of those who have experienced discrimination and harassment to define the behaviors that constitute harassment. The "reasonable man" standard has long been followed in the common law; it has been difficult, however, to establish a parallel "reasonable woman" standard for areas such as sexual harassment. Efforts to build academic climates that are more free from harassment and discrimination—racism, sexism, and homophobia—have been characterized as attacks on the valued tradition of academic freedom and the role of the university as a place for the free exchange of ideas. Some faculty may react to serious efforts to promote recognition of sexual harassment issues, greater publicity about students' options, and increased openness in discussing the issues as attacks on their prerogatives as teachers or their freedom to relate to students.

The valuable tradition of academic freedom is firmly established as a mechanism to protect faculty rights of free speech on political and social issues. It was never intended, however, to allow faculty to abuse the basic civil and human rights of students. Policies prohibiting racial, sexual preference, or gender-based harassment do not impinge on academic freedom. Instead they extend the privilege to students—allowing them to speak their own views in a free marketplace of ideas and to be treated with equality when they do. The basic intent of nondiscriminatory and sexual harassment policies is to prevent behavior in the academic community that is demeaning to students because of characteristics of their personhood—their gender, their race, or their sexual orientation. Such policies, and larger proposals to improve organizational climates and to maximize the goals of learning, ask faculty to increase their sensitivity to students and their learning needs, to respect students as being equal before the law, and to evidence respect for that long-sought equality.

A Second Type of Backlash Reaction

The second backlash reaction dismisses sexually harassing behavior that does not fit the strictest legal criteria. There is no question that sexual harassment has many complex legal implications and that policies against sexual harassment are based upon legal definitions of discrimination. Nevertheless, sexual harassment is not solely a legal issue; it is also a personal and social issue that affects an individual's and community's sense of safety and justice, as well as their ability to function. In social work, concern for the issue of sexual harassment is also a component of our professional ethics. Thus, it is important for social work administrators and faculty to realize that sexually harassing behavior does not have to fit the strictest legal definition of sexual harassment to be in violation of our code of ethics. We cannot simply dismiss, ignore, or minimize the impact of a damaging incident that does not meet the legal definition. Instances of inappropriate behavior pose ethical dilemmas, even if they are not legally actionable, and administrators should implement a secondary preventive or mediative strategy to handle such behavior. Thus, all incidents of harassment, whether they constitute occasional inappropriate remarks or ongoing physical or verbal abuse, must be addressed by administrators with equal rapidity, empathy, and fairness. To do less would violate the ethics and values of the profession.

Despite the discomfort or tension created by reactions intended to derail or dismiss the value of anti-harassment policies, academic administrators must maintain the stance that sexual harassment, like racial harassment, will not be tolerated under *any* conditions. Administrators should also, however, acknowledge and find ways to ameliorate the intensity of feeling that can be aroused in all community members by incidents, allegations, or simply discussion of sexual harassment. As Terry Singer illustrates in chapter 4, the costs of harassment ripple throughout the system, beyond the central costs for the accuser and the accused. When allegations of harassment are made, fairness and careful adherence to soundly developed policies and procedures are the best approach—although system-wide reverberations are inevitable, whatever the approach or outcome. To reduce system-wide costs, administrators should develop strategies to prevent harassment through education and discussion. Opportunities should be created that allow faculty, staff, and students to talk openly about the issue and the feelings it provokes, without defensiveness or animosity.

Harassment and Issues of Difference

Although some behavior can be identified as harassing by any reasonable observer, many situations arise in which a particular style of communication or choice of words may be interpreted by members of one cultural, racial, or gender group as demeaning or harassing when the conscious intent of the speaker was not offensive. Tannen (1990) presents an excellent analysis of typical communication failures between men and women, attributing these to the historical inequity of social power rooted in communication patterns between men and women. Kochman (1983), among others, has provided an interesting analysis of ways in which cultural patterns of speech between men and women within the same racial group can become problematic when they surface in communication between women and men of different racial backgrounds. Discussions of these patterns can help to identify problematic areas and to clarify ways to establish consensual standards for respectful communication in an organization. Some traditional patterns of communication, especially those based in social dominance or position power, can contribute to harassing situations. Faculty and administrators who have not felt inclined or been required to examine the impact of their behavior on those in subordinate positions may feel extremely uncomfortable at being asked to consider issues of potential abuse of status and power, and they may react in a variety of intense and defensive ways. Although it is important to illustrate the reasons that examination and change are needed, it is also important to acknowledge and allow for the expression of chagrin, frustration, or fear. The development of sexual harassment legislation from discrimination statutes in Title VII and case law did not arise from narrowly puritanical views of social behavior between men and women. Rather, it grew from the record of harassment and harm endured by women and others in less powerful positions than their harassers. The current spate of emotional reactions to increased attention to sexual harassment can occlude recognition of this history and documentation.

To diffuse the intensity of feeling, it may be helpful to view the issues raised by sexual harassment in the larger context of how change takes place within organizations. Understanding recent shifts in the historical operation of racism and sexism in our society is a starting point. Changes as fundamental as new roles for and norms of expected behavior between men and women will inevitably cause conflict. And the potential for conflict is heightened by other related social changes such as economic insecurity and increased racial and gender diversity at all levels in the workplace. With more women and men of color advancing in the academy, organizational strife will be common until a new, more egalitarian equilibrium is reached. As our society slowly achieves greater racial and gender equality, and as we find positive means to deal with increased diversity, the tension and strife will dissipate.

Schools of social work should be in the vanguard of our society in terms of analyzing these issues and developing mediative, ethical solutions. The next generations of social workers need to be educated in ways that will enable them to deal with and reduce the serious issues of sexism, racism, and homophobia in our society. For our students to be able to take on this challenge, they will need educational experiences and environments that promote equality and that do not countenance the abuses of power that are inherent in racism and sexism. Although in itself not sufficient to resolve the present tensions, understanding the change process can be helpful as faculty, staff, and students struggle to deal with differences and the development of more egalitarian norms.

Creating a Positive Environment

To create an environment in which faculty, staff, and students can safely and openly discuss issues raised by sexual harassment is to model the kind of professional practice in which we would want to engage. Deans, directors, faculty members, and field educators face the challenge and responsibility to create and sustain environments of safe learning, teaching, and practice and to develop positive problem-solving models. Creating learning environments that are more safe for students does not imply abandoning the academic responsibility to promote intellectual challenge, high standards of performance, a multiplicity of views, and argument in discourse. Those challenges are inherent in learning. In professional programs, students should be challenged to test social interventions, to question methods of practice and research, and to build knowledge. They should not, however, be expected to carry out these intellectual challenges in an environment or a specific situation in which they may be demeaned because of their gender or race.

A Safe Learning Environment

Creating a community free of sexual harassment demands action in a number of areas. First, safety can be enhanced through institutionalized efforts to educate all members of the school community about the definitions of sexual harassment and the issues surrounding it, about relevant academic and field policies, and about the consequences for those involved in harassment. As noted in the preceding chapters, the development of a policy against harassment, ongoing training for faculty and students, orientations for field faculty, presentations at student orientations, training and discussions in field settings, posters, letters from the dean/director, and newsletter articles can all convey the school's commitment to creating a safe learning environment in which harassment is less likely to occur.

Despite such preventive initiatives, however, instances of harassment undoubtedly will arise. When they do, the dean/director must ensure protection of the victim and confidentiality of all parties. This will be easier if both the victim and alleged harasser know their rights and understand the steps involved in the complaint process—in particular, that the victim is allowed to be "in the driver's seat" until the process reaches the stages of formal complaint.

A Positive Problem-Solving Model

A guiding principle in most problem-solving models is to first address problems at the lowest possible level. Problem solving with the principle of least contest may be used to keep the resolution at the lowest and most informal administrative level. Where such problem solving works—that is, where it stops the harassment and meets the concerns and safety needs of the person reporting harassment—it can mitigate some of the institutional involvements and costs. It must be remembered that students have a choice about where they first report. In many instances, problem solving at the lowest level means that mediative mechanisms within the school or department of social work should be used to resolve issues of harassment. However, incidents of harassment often must be reported to the central academic administration, and in that sense are automatically "kicked up" to a higher level. In any case, it is essential that the problem-solving model—that is, the steps for attempting to resolve harassment complaints—are clear, visible, and available to all members of the school community.

Opportunities for Open Dialogue

As previously noted, the intense feelings raised by issues of harassment should not be "pushed underground." Rather, all members of the school community should have available a variety of forums in which they feel safe to share their feelings and experiences. Given the power and status differences inherent in an academic community, this may entail establishing separate formats for faculty, staff, and students. It is quite feasible to build in such opportunities on a yearly basis in student government or women's caucus meetings, in staff meetings where university and school policies are presented and discussed, and in a variety of faculty formats for discussion of policies, the learning environment, and other related concerns. Faculty feeling threatened by the changes represented by the increased visibility given to sexual harassment need a setting in which they can openly express their uncertainties and anxieties. Staff and students need an opportunity to discuss issues related to harassment and to sound out the seriousness of policies, procedures, and administrative commitment. Opportunities to talk through some of these mixed feelings are essential to creating positive work and learning environments.

Such forums for dialogue should be developed with the recognition that sexual harassment is interconnected with other issues raised in increasingly diverse faculty and student bodies. The models that we develop for positively addressing sexual harassment can provide guidance on how to deal with other types of harassing and discriminatory behavior. These discussions can help to strengthen classroom and field presentations about issues of equality, respect for the individual and other social work values. On the other hand, as noted by Michael Reisch, it is important to avoid the creation of a "hierarchy of oppression," in which racism and sexism are set up as dichotomies, or in which potential allies are turned against one another through unnecessary competition around their relative merits as victims of discrimination. Nor should attention to other types of harassing and discriminatory behavior be used to dilute the significance of sexual harassment in itself, as something that "just happens to a few women" or as "not a big deal." As shown throughout this volume, it is a serious reality in academic and field settings and can cause substantial harm.

Implications for Social Work Education

Attention to building learning environments that provide safety, ensure egalitarian treatment regardless of class, race, gender, or sexual orientation, promote opportunities for discussion of discrimination and harassment, and develop positive problem-solving methods are key strategies for social work education both to model professional values and practice and to provide students with tools to fight discrimination in the larger society. It is important that schools and departments take up this challenge.

This volume is intended to assist faculties, administrators, and students of schools of social work in building more positive learning environments that can help to prevent problems of discrimination and harassment. To make best use of this work, school leaders should consider issues raised in each chapter and develop appropriate action guidelines. It is important for students, staff, faculty, and especially administrators responsible for dealing with issues of harassment to understand the legal definitions, statutory and case law, and frameworks for policy development. Where it has not been done, establishment of a task force or committee to examine sexual harassment policies and the learning environment should be undertaken. Barbara Shank provides a timely and scholarly presentation of policy issues that will be valuable in these considerations. It is also important, however, that deans/directors and faculty committee members recognize that new case and statutory law will emerge, that they should keep informed of any new legal precedents, and that they should work with their college or university attorney to integrate the social work policy with the institution's overall policies on harassment and discrimination.

As noted by Deborah Valentine and colleagues, it is critically important that schools and departments of social work develop a specific policy for students in field placements, that schools encourage field agencies to develop their own policies, and that orientation and training for field faculty about sexual harassment policies become basic components of the school or department's yearly cycle. Students are extremely vulnerable in field placements and many schools, without realizing it, may not have adequate policies and mechanisms in place to protect them. Efforts must be made by all schools and departments to address this issue. In both academic and agency field settings, leaders need to identify and keep abreast of relevant state law on workplace discrimination and harassment.

Review of the basic research on sexual harassment in schools and in field settings (Singer; Valentine et al.) gives clear indication that sexual harassment is a concern for social work education. Terry Singer's analysis of the human and institutional costs of harassment should be carefully examined. Schools should consider these individual and systemic costs both in terms of designing strategies for prevention and procedures for handling harassment cases. Michael Reisch's and Nancy Hooyman and Lorraine Gutiérrez's chapters present strategies for administrators to use in developing safer environments and strategies for prevention of sexual harassment. Their recommendations can be adapted to the needs of particular schools and departments and serve as the basis for specific action guidelines.

In addition to the strategies and models presented in earlier chapters, the volume's bibliography and appendices are intended to help individual departments and schools design sexual harassment policies, procedures, and prevention strategies appropriate to their own setting. The bibliography includes a comprehensive set of references on sexual harassment that will be useful in further analysis and investigation of these issues.

Appendix A presents the sexual harassment policies developed at the University of Washington, the College of St. Catherine/University of St. Thomas, and San Francisco State University, with the program materials from the University of North Carolina at Chapel Hill. These are strong representative policies that can serve as useful starting points or models for other schools to develop or revise their own policies. The policies provide the universities' definitions of sexual harassment, outline its prohibition on campus, and delineate procedures for reporting, processing, and adjudicating harassment incidents.

The model Field Policy developed by the University of South Carolina is presented in Appendix B. This policy should be of considerable assistance to the many schools and departments that have not yet developed a policy to protect students in field settings. As Valentine and colleagues note, only 21% of schools report that they maintain a policy that protects students in field placements. Furthermore, the authors note that standard university or college policies aimed at issues of harassment on campus may not be considered legally binding or protective of students in the field. Schools of social work need to examine their own policies and revise them accordingly.

The training materials provided in Appendix C were developed at the College of St. Catherine/University of St. Thomas and at the University of Washington. The intent of the administrators and faculty who designed them was to provide basic information about sexual harassment issues and to initiate preventive education strategies. Some items can be used as posters to heighten awareness of discrimination/harassment issues and to publicize program policies and reporting procedures. Most important, these materials can be used as the basis for developing training materials for students, staff, and faculty in any social work education program. Some materials will be particularly useful in focusing discussion and planning for strategies to diminish and prevent harassment. Items are included that describe "trigger incidents" useful in promoting both discussion on why or whether specific incidents are harassing and analysis of how program policies might apply to the situations. These trigger incidents may also be used to clarify definitions and the range of behaviors that can be perceived as harassment or discrimination based on gender, race, or sexual orientation.

Some materials present definitions and policy points; others explore responses, identify resources, or describe reporting procedures and the process of handling and adjudicating reports. Programs should add materials that illustrate their own definitions, policies, reporting procedures, resources for support, and individual and institutional means for dealing with incidents of sexual harassment. These materials could easily be incorporated into larger scale presentations that cover program policies and processes for dealing with discrimination or harassment incidents related to race, gender, and sexual orientation. While there is still very little literature on responses to sexual harassment in academic and social work field settings, there is a growing body of literature about sexual harassment in the workplace. Several recent handbooks provide valuable general guidelines for understanding sexual harassment, the relevant law and case precedents, and both individual and systemic approaches to stopping harassment (Bravo & Cassedy, 1992; Colatosti & Karg, 1992; Petrocelli & Repa, 1992; Wagner, 1992; and Webb, 1992).

In combination, the chapters, research studies, bibliography, and training materials should assist programs in their efforts to plan and implement stronger policies and procedures and to develop preventive strategies to curtail sexual harassment in social work education.

References

Bravo, E., & Cassedy, E. (1992). *The 9 to 5 guide to combating sexual harassment: Candid advice from 9 to 5—the National Association of Working Women.* New York: John Wiley & Sons.

Cohen, L. R. (1992). Legal definitions of sexual harassment are too broad. In C. Wekesser, K. L. Swisher, & C. Pierce (Eds.), *Sexual harassment.* San Diego: Greenhaven Press.

Colatosti, C., & Karg, E. (1992). *STOPping sexual harassment: A handbook for union and workplace activists.* Available from Labor Notes, 7435 Michigan Ave., Detroit MI 48210.

Davidson, N. (1992). Feminist legal definitions of sexual harassment will result in injustice. In C. Wekesser, K. L. Swisher, & C. Pierce (Eds.), *Sexual harassment.* San Diego: Greenhaven Press.

Faludi, S. (1993, October 25). Whose hype? *Newsweek, CXXII*(17), 61.

Kantrowitz, B. (1992). Sexual harassment in America: An overview. In C. Wekesser, K. Swisher, & C. Pierce (Eds.), *Sexual harassment.* San Diego: Greenhaven Press.

Kochman, T. (1983). *Black and white styles in conflict.* Chicago: University of Chicago Press.

Leo, J. (1992). Broad legal definitions of sexual harassment threaten men. In C. Wekesser, K. L. Swisher, & C. Pierce (Eds.), *Sexual harassment.* San Diego: Greenhaven Press.

Meritor Savings Bank v. Vinson, 477 U.S. 57 (1986).

Morrison, T. (Ed.). (1992). *Race-ing justice, en-gendering power: Essays on Anita Hill, Clarence Thomas, and the construction of social reality.* New York: Pantheon Books.

Petrocelli, W., & Repa, B. K. (1992). *Sexual harassment on the job: What it is and how to stop it.* Berkeley, CA: Nolo Press.

Robertson, C., Dyer, C., & Campbell, D. (1985). *Report on a survey of sexual harassment policies and procedures.* (Report prepared by the Office for Women's Affairs) Bloomington: Indiana University.

Roscoe, B., Goodwin, M. P., Repp, S. E., & Rose, M. (1987). Sexual harassment of university students and student employees: Findings and implications. *College Student Journal, 21*(3), 254-273.

Schneider, B. E. (1987). Graduate women, sexual harassment, and university policy. *Journal of Higher Education, 58*(1), 46-65.

Tannen, D. (1990). *You just don't understand: Women and men in conversation.* New York: Ballantine.

Wagner, E. J. (1992). *Sexual harassment in the workplace: How to prevent, investigate, and resolve problems in your organization.* New York: AMACOM American Management Association.

Webb, S. L. (1992). *Step forward: Sexual harassment in the workplace: What you need to know!* New York: MasterMedia.

Weiss, M. (1992). Sexual harassment definitions discriminate against men. In C. Wekesser, K. L. Swisher, & C. Pierce (Eds.), *Sexual harassment.* San Diego: Greenhaven Press.

CSWE Women's Commission Selected Bibliography on Sexual Harassment

compiled by Beverly Koerin and Marie Weil

Documents on Sexual Harassment

A

Abrams, K. (1989). Gender discrimination and the transformation of workplace norms. *Vanderbilt Law Review, 42*, 1183-1248.

Adams, A. & Abarbanel, G. (1988). *Sexual assault on campus: What colleges can do.* Santa Monica, CA: Santa Monica Hospital Medical Center.

Adams, J.W., Kottke, J.L., & Padgitt, J.S. (1983). Sexual harassment of university students. *Journal of College Student Personnel, 24*(6), 484-490.

Agencies no haven. (1984, April). *NASW News.*

Alexander v. Yale University, 631 F. 2d 178 (2nd Cir. 1980).

Allen, D. & Okawa, J.B. (1987, Winter). A counseling center looks at sexual harassment. *Journal of the National Association for Women Deans, Administrators, and Counselors, 50* , 9-16.

American Association of University Professors. (1983). Suggested policy and procedures for handling complaints. *Academe, 69*(2), 15a-16a.

Analysis of Recent Supreme Court Ruling. (1981, April/May). *WOW news focus.*

Anderson, K.S. (1987). Employer liability under Title VII for sexual harassment after *Meritor Savings Bank vs. Vinson. Columbia Law Review, 87,* 1258-1279.

Annotated bibliography on sexual harassment in education. (1982). *Women's Rights Law Reporter, 7*(2).

A resource manual on sexual harassment. (1982). Concord, NH: New Hampshire Commission on the Status of Women.

Backhouse, D. & Cohen, L. (1981). *Sexual harassment on the job.* Englewood Cliffs, NJ: Prentice-Hall.

Baxter, R.H., Jr., & Hermle, L.C. (1989). *Sexual harassment in the workplace* (3rd ed.). New York: Executive Enterprises Publications.

Bennett, M. & Bennett, J. (1973). D.I.E. Modification of "Descriptions, Inference, Judgment" distinction in Korzibsky. *Science and sanity.*

Benson, D.J. & Thomson, G.E. (1982). Sexual harassment on a university campus: The confluence of authority relations, sexual interest and gender stratification. *Social Problems, 29,* 236-252.

Beauvais, K. (1986). Workshops to combat sexual harassment: A case study of changing attitudes. *Signs, 12,* 130-145.

Bernays, A. (1981). *Professor Romeo.* New York: Weidenfeld and Nicolson.

Blanashan, S.A. (1983). Activitism, research, and policy: Sexual harassment. *Journal of the National Association for Women Deans, Administrators, and Counselors, 46*(2), 16-22.

Blonston, G. & Scanlan, C. (1991, October 12). Hearing depicts war of sexes in workplace. *The State.* [Columbia, SC], pp. 1A, 7A.

Brandenburg, J.B. (1982). Sexual harassment in the university: Guidelines for establishing a grievance procedure. *Signs, 8*(2), 320-336.

Bravo, E. & Cassedy, E. (1992). *The 9 to 5 guide to combating sexual harassment: Candid advice from 9 to 5 - the National Association of Working Women.* New York: John Wiley & Sons.

Brownmiller, G. & Alexander, D. (1992). From Carmita Wood to Anita Hill. *Ms., 2*(4), 70-71.

Bularzik, M. (1978, July-August). Sexual harassment at the workplace: Historical notes. *Radical American, 12,* 25-43.

C

Campbell, D. (1984). Sexual harassment in education. Information for Indiana University faculty, staff and students provided by Office for Women's Affairs.

Carroll, L. & Ellis, K.L. (1989). Faculty attitudes towards sexual harassment: Survey results, survey process. *Journal of the National Association for Women Deans, Administrators, and Counselors, 52*(3), 35-42.

Chuddle, C. & Nesvold, B. (1985). Administrative risk and sexual harassment: Legal and ethical responsibilities on campus. *Political Studies, 33,* 780-789.

Co-employee's liability for sexual harassment different from employer's liability. (1981, August). *Equal employment compliance update.*

Cohen, L.R. (1992). Legal definitions of sexual harassment are too broad. In C. Wekesser, K.L. Swisher, & C. Pierce (Eds.), *Sexual harassment.* San Diego: Greenhaven Press.

Colatosti, C. & Karg, E. (1992). *STOPping sexual harassment: A handbook for union and workplace activists.* Available from Labor Notes, 7435 Michigan Ave., Detroit, MI 48210.

Cole, E.K. (Ed.). (1990). *Sexual harassment on campus: A legal compendium.* Presented at the Stetson College of Law Ninth Annual Conference on Law and Higher Education. National Association of College and University Attorneys.

Cole, E.K. (1986). Recent legal developments in sexual harassment. *Journal of College and University Law, 13,* 267-284.

Coles, F.S. (1986). Forced to quit: Sexual harassment complaint and agency response. *Sex Roles, 14*(1-2), 81-95.

Collins, E.G.C. & Blodgett, T.B. (1981, March-April). Sexual harassment . . . Some see it . . . Some won't. *Harvard Business Review,* 77-95.

Comment. (1989). Defining hostile work environment under Title VII. *Western New England Law Review, 11,* 143-177.

Comment. (1976). Employment discrimination—Sexual harassment and Title VII. *New York University Law Review, 51,* 148-167.

Connolly, W.B., Jr. & Marshall, A.B. (1989). Sexual harassment of university or college students by faculty members. *Journal of College and University Law, 15,* 381-403.

Conroe, R., Brandstetter, J., Brown, M., DeMarinis, V., & Loeffler, D. (1986). *Sexual harassment in the clinical supervision of students: An overview and suggested guidelines.* Paper prepared by the Supervision Subcommittee, Training Institutions Work Group, Task Force on Sexual Exploitation by Counselors and Therapists.

Craib, R. (1977, July 22). Sex and women at UC Berkeley—Two surveys. *San Francisco Chronicle.*

Crocker, P.L. (1983). An analysis of university definitions of sexual harassment. *Signs, 8,* 696-707.

Crull, P. (1982, July). Stress effects of sexual harassment on the job: Implications for counseling. *American Journal of Orthopsychiatry, 52,* 539-543.

Crull, P. (1979, Fall). *The impact of sexual harassment on the job: A profile of the experiences of 92 women.* Research Series, Report No. 3 (New York: Working Women's Institute). Also see, Working Women's Institute, *Sexual harassment on the job: Questions and answers.* (New York: Working Women's Institute, 1978).

D

Daily, D.M. (1980, January). Are social workers sexist? A replication. *Social Work, 25,* 46-50.

Davidson, N. (1992). Feminist legal definitions of sexual harassment will result in injustice. In C. Wekesser, K.L. Swisher, & C. Pierce (Eds.), *Sexual harassment.* San Diego: Greenhaven Press.

Deane, N.H. & Tillar, D.L. (1981). *Sexual harassment: An employment issue.* Washington, DC: College and University Personnel Association.

DeChiara, P. (1988). The need for universities to have rules on consensual sexual relationships between faculty members and students. *Columbia Journal of Law and Social Problems, 21,* 137-162.

Dziech, B.W. & Weiner, L. (1984). *The lecherous professor: Sexual harassment on campus*. Boston: Beacon Press.

E

Ecabert, G. (1987). An employer's guide to understanding liability for sexual harassment under Title VII: *Meritor Savings Bank v. Vinson*. *University of Cincinnati Law Review, 55*, 1181.

Ehrhart, J.K. & Sandler, B.R. (1985). *Campus gang rape: Party games?* Washington, DC: Project on the Status and Education of Women, Association of American Colleges.

Equal Employment Opportunity Commission. (1980). Questions and answers. *Equal Employment Opportunity Today, 7*, 1.

Equal Employment Opportunity Commission. (1980). Guidelines on discrimination because of sex, Title VII, section 703. *Federal Register, 45*.

Equal Employment Opportunity Commission. (1980). *Sexual harassment guidelines*. (29 CFR, Chapter XIV, Part 1604, 11a). Washington, DC: U.S. Government Printing Office.

F

Faley, R.H. (1982). Sexual harassment: Critical review of legal cases with general principles and preventive measures. *Personnel Psychology, 35*, 583-600.

Farley, L. (1978). *Sexual shakedown: The sexual harassment of women on the job*. New York: McGraw-Hill.

Faludi, S. (1991). *Backlash: The undeclared war against American women*. New York: Crown.

Faludi, S. (1993, October 25). Whose hype? *Newsweek, CXXII*(17), 61.

Fighting sexual harassment: An advocacy handbook. (1979). Cambridge, MA: Alliance Against Sexual Coercion.

Fishbein, E.A. (1982). *Sexual harassment: Practice guidance for handling a new issue on campus*. Baltimore: Johns Hopkins University.

Fitzgerald, L.F., Weitzman, L.M., Gold, Y., & Ormerod, M. (1988). Academic harassment: Sex and denial in scholarly garb. *Psychology of Women Quarterly, 12,* 329-340.

Franklin, P., Moglen, H., Zatlin-Borging, P., & Angress, R. (1981). *Sexual and gender harassment in the academy.* New York: The Modern Language Association of America.

G

Gartland, P.A. & Bevilacqua, W. (1983). Sexual harassment: Recent research and useful resources. *Journal of the National Association for Women Deans, Administrators, and Counselors, 46*(2), 47-50.

Garvey, M. (1986). The high cost of sexual harassment suits. *Personnel Journal, 65*(1), 75-80.

Gibbs, A. & Balthrope, R.B. (1982, March). Sexual harassment in the workplace and its ramifications for academia. *Journal of College Student Personnel,* 158-162.

Gite, L. (1982, April/May). Black women workplace problems: Sexual harassment and racial discrimination. *The Black Collegian,* 44-47.

Glaser, R. & Thorpe, J. (1986). Unethical intimacy: A survey of sexual contact and advances between psychology educators and female graduate students. *American Psychologist, 41,* 43-51.

Goldberg, A. (1978, May). Sexual harassment and Title VII: The foundation for the elimination of sexual cooperation as an employment condition. *Michigan Law Review, 76,* 1007-1035.

Goodwin, M.P., Roscoe, B., Rose, M., & Repp, S.E. (1989). Sexual harassment: Experiences of university employees. *Journal of the National Association for Women Deans, Administrators, and Counselors, 52*(3), 25-33.

Greene, S.A. (1988). Reevaluation of Title VII abusive environment claims based on sexual harassment. *Thurgood Marshall Law Review, 13,* 29-65.

Gruber, J.E. & Bjorn, L. (1982, August). Blue collar blues: The sexual harassment of women auto workers. *Work and Occupations, 9,* 271-299.

H

Harris v. Forklift Systems, Inc. 114 S. Ct. 367 (1993).

Heller, S. (1986). 1 in 6 female students in psychology reports having sexual contact with a professor. *Chronicle of Higher Education, 31,* 23.

Henley, N. (1973). Power, sex and nonverbal communication. In B. Thorne & N. Henley (Eds.), *Language and sex: Difference and dominance* (184-203). Rowley, MA: Newbury House.

Hill, A. (1992). The nature of the beast. *Ms., 2*(4), 32-33.

Hoffman, F.L. (1986). Sexual harassment in academia: Feminist theory and institutional practice. *Harvard Educational Review, 56*(2), 105-121.

Hughes, J.O. & Sandler, B.R. (1986). *In case of sexual harassment—A guide for women students.* Washington, DC: Project on the Status and Education of Women, Association of American Colleges.

J

James, J. (1981, Winter). Sexual harassment. *Public Personnel Management Journal,* 402-407.

Jensen, I.W. & Gutek, B.A. (1982). Attributions and assignments of responsibility in sexual harassment. *Journal of Social Issues, 38*(4), 121-136.

Johnson, P. (1976). Women and power: Toward a theory of effectiveness. *Journal of Social Issues, 32*(3), 99-110.

K

Kandel, W.L. (1988). Sexual harassment: Persistent, prevalent, but preventable. *Employee Relations Law Journal, 14,* 439-451.

Kantrowitz, B. (1992). Sexual harassment in America: An overview. In C. Wekesser, K. Swisher, & C. Pierce (Eds.), *Sexual harassment.* San Diego: Greenhaven Press.

Kaplan, S.J. (1991). Consequences of sexual harassment in the workplace. *Affilia, 6*(3), 50-65.

Kardner, S. (1974). Sex and the physician-patient relationship. *American Journal of Psychiatry, 131,* 1134-1136.

Karsten, M.F. & Kramer, G.H. (1985, January). Perceptions of sexual harassment in higher education. Paper presented at the Women in Higher Education Conference, Orlando, FL.

Kaufman, S. & Wylie, M.L. (1983). One-session workshop on sexual harassment. *Journal of the National Association for Women Deans, Administrators, and Counselors, 46*(2), 39-42.

Keller, E. (1990, January/February). Consensual relationships and institutional policy. *Academe, 76*(1), 29-32.

Keller, E.A. (1988). Consensual amorous relationships between faculty and students: The constitutional right to privacy. *Journal of College and University Law, 15,* 21-42.

Kenig, S. & Ryan, J. (1986). Sex differences in levels of tolerance and attribution of blame for sexual harassment on a university campus. *Sex Roles, 15,* 535-549.

Kennevick, J. (1986). The significance of the *Vinson* decision on corporate employees. *Journal of Contemporary Law, 12,* 163.

Kent State University. Elements of sexual harassment. Unpublished manuscript, Office of Affirmative Action, Kent, Ohio.

Kirst-Ashman, K.K. (1985, January). *Confronting sexual harassment: Implementation of a university sexual harassment awareness program.* Paper presented at the Council on Social Work Education Annual Program Meeting, Washington, DC.

Kochman, T. (1983). *Black and white styles in conflict.* Chicago: University of Chicago Press.

Konrad, A.M. & Gutek, B.A. (1986). Impact of work experiences on attitudes towards sexual harassment. *Administrative Science Quarterly, 31,* 422-438.

L

Legal remedies for sexual harassment. (1983). Washington, DC: Women's Legal Defense Fund.

Leo, J. (1992). Broad legal definitions of sexual harassment threaten men. In C. Wekesser, K.L. Swisher, & C. Pierce (Eds.), *Sexual harassment.* San Diego: Greenhaven Press.

Livingston, J.A. (1982). Response to sexual harassment on the job: Legal, organizational and individual actions. *Journal of Social Issues, 38*(4), 5-22.

Longstreth, L.B. (1987). Hostile environment sexual harassment: A wrong without a remedy?—*Meritor Savings Bank vs. Vinson. Suffolk University Law Review, 21,* 811-829.

Lott, B., Reilly, M.E., & Harvard, D. (1982). Sexual assault and harassment: A campus community case study. *Signs, 8,* 296-319.

MacKinnon, C.A. (1979). *Sexual harassment of working women: A case of sex discrimination.* New Haven, CT: Yale University Press.

Maihoff, N. & Forest, L. (1983). Sexual harassment in higher education: An assessment study. *Journal of the National Association for Women Deans, Administrators, and Counselors, 46*(2), 3-8.

Manemann, M.C. (1989). The meaning of 'sex' in Title VII: Is favoring an employee lover a violation of the act? *Northwestern University Law Review, 83,* 612-664.

Maypole, D.E. (1986). Sexual harassment of social workers at work: Injustice within? *Social Work, 31*(1), 29-34.

Maypole, D.E. & Skaine, R. (1982, December). Sexual harassment of blue collar workers. *Journal of Sociology and Social Welfare, 9,* 682-695.

Maypole, D.E. & Skaine, R. (1983). Sexual harassment in the workplace. *Social Work, 28*(5), 385-390.

Mazer, D.B. & Percival, E.F. (1989). Ideology or experience? The relationships among perceptions, attitudes, and experiences of sexual harassment in university students. *Sex Roles, 20,* 135-147.

McCarthy, M.M. (1987). The developing law pertaining to sexual harassment. *Education Law Reporter, 36,* 7-14.

McGaghy, M.D. (1985). *Sexual harassment: A guide to resources.* Boston: G.K. Hall.

Meek, P.M. & Lynch, A.Q. (1983). Establishing an informal grievance procedure for cases of sexual harassment of students. *Journal of the National Association for Women Deans, Administrators, and Counselors, 46*(2), 30-33.

Merit System Protection Board. (1981). *Sexual harassment in the federal workplace: Is it a problem?* Washington, DC: Office of Merit System Review and Studies.

Metha, A. & Nigg, J. (1983). Sexual harassment on campus: An institutional response. *Journal of the National Association for Women Deans, Administrators, and Counselors, 46*(2), 9-15.

Meyer, M., Oestriech, J., Collins, F., & Berchtold, I. (1981). *Sexual harassment.* New York: Petrocelli Books.

Middletown, L. (1980, September). Sexual harassment by professors: An increasingly visible problem. *Chronicle of Higher Education, 1,* 4-5.

Montgomery, A. (1978). Issues in therapist training and supervision. *Psychology, 15,* 28-36.

Morrison, T. (Ed.). (1992). *Race-ing justice, en-gendering power: Essays on Anita Hill, Clarence Thomas, and the construction of social reality.* New York: Pantheon Books.

Munich, A. (1978, February). Seduction in academe. *Psychology Today, 82,* 82-84, 108

Neale, N.C., Paige, R.M., & Thomas, K. (1989). *The wrong idea: A cross-cultural training program about sexual harassment.* Office of International Education, University of Minnesota.

Neugarten, D.A. & Shafritz, J.M. (Eds.). (1978). *Sexuality in organizations: Romantic and coercive behaviors at work.* Oak Park, IL: Moore Publishing Co.

Nowlin, W.A. (1988, December). Sexual harassment in the workplace: How arbitrators rule. *Arbitration Journal, 43,* 31-40.

O

Olson, C. & McKinney, K. (1989). Processes inhibiting the reduction of sexual harassment in academe: Alternative explanation. *Journal of the National Association for Women Deans, Administrators, and Counselors, 52*(3), 7-14.

Omilian, S. (1986). *What every employer should be doing about sexual harassment.* Madison, CT: Business and Legal Reports.

P

Padgitt, S.C. & Padgitt, J.S. (1986). Cognitive structure of sexual harassment: Implications for university policy. *Journal of College Student Personnel, 27,* 34-39.

Paige, R.M. & Martin, J.N. (1983). Ethical issues and ethics in cross-cultural training. In D. Landis & R.W. Brislin (Eds.), *Handbook of intercultural training: Issues in theory and design, Vol. 1* (36-60). New York: Pergamon.

Paludi, M.A. (1991). *Ivory power: Sexual harassment on campus.* New York: State University of New York Press.

Paludi, M.A. & DeFour, D.C. (1989). Research on sexual harassment in the academy: Definitions, findings, constraints, responses. *Journal of the National Association for Women Deans, Administrators, and Counselors, 52*(3), 43-48.

Peer harassment: Hassles for women on campus. (1988). Washington, DC: Project on the Status and Education of Women, Association of American Colleges.

Perry, S. (1983, March). Sexual harassment on the campuses: Deciding where to draw the line. *Chronicle of Higher Education,* 21-22.

Petrocelli, W. & Repa, B.K. (1992). *Sexual harassment on the job: What it is and how to stop it.* Berkeley, CA: Nolo Press.

Polakoff, S.E. (1984). A plan for coping with sexual harassment. *Journal of College Student Personnel, 25*(2), 165-167.

Pollack, W. (1990). Sexual harassment: Women's experience vs. legal definitions. *Harvard Women's Law Journal, 13,* 35-85.

Pope, K., Keith-Spiegel, P., & Tabachnick, B. (1986, February). Sexual attraction to clients. *American Psychologist, 41(2),* 147-157.

Pope, K., Levenson, H., & Schover, L. (1979). Sexual intimacy in psychology training: Results and implications of a national survey. *American Psychologist, 34,* 682-689.

Pope, K., Schover, L., & Levenson, H. (1980). Sexual behavior between clinical supervisors and trainees: Implications for professional standards. *Professional Psychology, 11,* 157-162.

Project on the Status of Women. (1979). *On campus with women.* Washington, DC: Association of American Colleges.

Project on the Status and Education of Women. (1978). *Sexual harassment.* Washington, DC: Association of American Colleges.

Reid, P.C. (1981). *Dealing with sexual harassment.* New York: Management Resources, Inc.

Reilly, M.E., Lott, B., & Gallogly, S.M. (1986). Sexual harassment of university students. *Sex Roles, 15,* 333-358.

Reilly, T., Carpenter, S., Dull, V., & Bartlett, K. (1982). The factorial survey: An approach to defining sexual harassment on campus. *Journal of Social Issues, 38*(4), 99-110.

Renick, J.C. (1980, August). Sexual harassment at work: Why it happens, what to do about it. *Personnel Journal, 59,* 658-662.

Robertson, C., Dyer, C.E., & Campbell, D. (1985). *Report on survey of sexual harassment policies and procedures.* Office for Women's Affairs, Bloomington, IN: Indiana University.

Robertson, C., Dyer, C.E., & Campbell, D. (1988). Campus harassment: Sexual harassment policies and procedures at institutions of higher learning. *Signs, 13*(4), 792-812.

Roscoe, B., Goodwin, M.P., Repp, S.E., & Rose, M. (1987). Sexual harassment of university students and student employees: Findings and implications. *College Student Journal, 21*(3), 254-273.

Ross, C.S. & Green, V.A. (1983). Sexual harassment: A liability higher education must face. *Journal of the College and University Personnel Association, 34,* 1-9.

Rowe, M.P. (1981). Dealing with sexual harassment. *Harvard Business Review, 59,* 42-46.

S

Safran, C. (1976, November). What men do to women on the job: A shocking look at sexual harassment. *Redbook,* 217.

Sandler, B.R. (1981). Sexual harassment: A hidden problem. *Educational Record, 62*(1), 52-57.

Schneider, B.E. (1987). Graduate women, sexual harassment, and university policy. *The Journal of Higher Education, 58*(1), 46-65.

Schneider, R.G. (1987). Sexual harassment and higher education. *Texas Law Review, 65,* 525-583.

Schoener, G. (1986). *Administrative safeguards which limit the risk of sexual exploitation by psychotherapists.* Minneapolis: Walk-in Counseling Center, 55404.

Sexual harassment and labor relations: A special BNA report. (1981). Washington, DC: The Bureau of National Affairs, Inc.

Sexual harassment: A report on the sexual harassment of students. (1980). Washington, DC: National Advisory Council on Women's Educational Programs.

Sexual harassment: Issues and answers. (1986). Washington, DC: College and University Personnel Association.

Sexual harassment: It's not academic. (1982). Bethesda, MD: Miranda Associates, Inc.

Sexual harassment on campus. (1983). *Journal of the National Association of Women Deans, Administrators, and Counselors, 46,* 1-56.

Sexual harassment—Questions and answers. (1980, September). *The equal employment opportunity report, 372.*

Sexual harassment: What it is, what to do about it. (1980). Berkeley, CA: Women Organized Against Sexual Harassment.

Shaney, M.J. (1986). Perceptions of harm: The consent defense in sexual harassment cases. *Iowa Law Review, 71,* 1109.

Shank, B. & Johnson, N. (1986, March). *Sexual harassment: An issue for classroom and field educators.* Presented at the Annual Program Meeting of the Council on Social Work Education, Miami.

Shearer, R.A. (1989, Summer). Paramour claims under Title VII: Liability for co-worker/employer sexual relationships. *Employee Relations Law Journal, 15,* 57-66.

Shultz, J., Milillo, M., Couchman, J., & Lundeen, J. (1986). Using administrative procedures to prevent sexual exploitation by therapists and counselors. *The Minnesota exchange.* St. Paul, MN: Minnesota Program for Victims of Sexual Assault.

Simon, L.K. & Forrest, L. (1983). Implementing a policy at a large university. *Journal of the National Association for Women Deans, Administrators, and Counselors, 46*(2).

Somers, A. (1982). Sexual harassment in academe: Legal issues and definitions. *Journal of Social Issues, 38*(4), 23-32.

Somers, P.A. (1983). Sexual harassment and employment: Why college counselors should be concerned. *Journal of the National Association for Women Deans, Administrators, and Counselors, 46*(2).

State of Wisconsin's Fair Employment Act. (1983).

Stimpson, C.R. (1989). Over-reaching: Sexual harassment. *Journal of the National Association for Women Deans, Administrators, and Counselors, 52*(3), 1-6.

Stokes, J. (1983). Effective training programs: One institutional response to sexual harassment. *Journal of the National Association for Women Deans, Administrators, and Counselors, 46*(2).

Sullivan, M. & Bybee, D.I. (1987). Female students and sexual harassment: What factors predict reporting behavior? *Journal of the National Association for Women Deans, Administrators, and Counselors, 50*, 11-16.

Sutton, J.A. (1982, May). Sex discrimination among social workers. *Social Work, 27*, 211-217.

T

Tangri, S.S., Burt, M.R., & Johnson, L. (1982). Sexual harassment at work: Three explanatory models. *Journal of Social Issues, 38*(4), 33-54.

Tannen, D. (1990). *You just don't understand: Women and men in conversation.* New York: Ballantine.

Terpstra, D.E. & Baker, D.D. (1987). A hierarchy of sexual harassment. *Journal of Psychology, 121*, 599-607.

Till, F.J. (1980). *Sexual harassment: A report on the sexual harassment of students.* Washington, DC: The National Advisory Council on Women's Educational Programs.

Title VII of the Civil Rights Act of 1964, 42 U.S.C. Sec. 2000c-2000c-17.

Title IX of the Education Amendments of 1972, 20 U.S.C. Sec. 1681-1686.

Title IX: The half full, half empty glass. (1981). Washington, DC: National Advisory Council on Women's Education Programs.

Tuana, N. (1984). Sexual harassment in academe: Issues of power and coercion. *College Teaching, 33,* 53-63.

Tuana, N. (1985, Spring). Sexual harassment in academe. *College Testing, 33,* 53-64.

U.S. Merit Systems Protection Board. (1981, March). A Report of the U.S. Merit Systems Protection Board, Office of Merit Systems Review and Studies. *Sexual harassment in the federal workplace: Is it a problem?* Washington, DC: Government Printing Office.

University of Minnesota. (1984). *Sexual harassment.* (Available from the Office of Equal Opportunity and Affirmative Action, University of Minnesota, Minneapolis.)

Vhay, M.D. (1988). The harms of asking: Towards a comprehensive treatment of sexual harassment. *University of Chicago Law Review, 55,* 328-362.

Vinciguerra, M. (1989). The aftermath of *Meritor*: A search for standards in the law of sexual harassment. *Yale Law Journal, 98,* 1717-1738.

Wagner, E.J. (1992). *Sexual harassment in the workplace: How to prevent, investigate, and resolve problems in your organization.* New York: AMACOM American Management Association.

Walker, G., Erickson, L., & Woolsey, L. (1980, June). *Sexual harassment: Ethical research and clinical implications in the academic setting.* Paper presented at the Canadian Psychological Association Convention, Calgary, Alberta.

Webb, S.L. (1992). *Step forward: Sexual harassment in the workplace: What you need to know!* New York: Master Media.

Weber-Burden, E. & Rossi, P.H. (1982). Defining sexual harassment on campus: A replication and extension. *Journal of Social Issues, 38*(4), 111-120.

Weiss, M. (1992). Sexual harassment definitions discriminate against men. In C. Wekesser, K.L. Swisher, C. Pierce (Eds.), *Sexual harassment*. San Diego: Greenhaven Press.

Wekesser, C., Swisher, K.L., & Pierce, C. (Eds.). (1992). *Sexual harassment*. San Diego: Greenhaven Press.

White, W. (1986). *Incest in the organizational family*. Bloomington, IL: Lighthouse Training Institute.

Whitmore, R.L. (1983). *Sexual harassment at UC–Davis*. University of California Women's Resources and Research Center, 1-91.

Wilson, K.R. & Kraus, L.A. (1983). Sexual harassment in the university. *Journal of College Student Personnel, 24,* 219-224.

Wise, S. & Stanley, L. (1987). *Georgie Porgie: Sexual harassment in everyday life*. New York: Pandora.

Films on Sexual Harassment

Preventing Sexual Harassment.
(From the Fair Employment Practice Series).
BNA Communications Inc., 9439 Key West Avenue, Rockville, MD 20850.
Explores sexual harassment from innuendo to blatant attack, presenting vignettes based on actual cases. Points out management responsibilities and employee rights, provides guidelines for dealing with incidents involving sexual harassment, emphasizes the need to act promptly and correctly, and stresses the importance of practicing the principles of good management to prevent such incidents in the first place.

Fair Employment Practice Program.
Outstanding EEO Multimedia Program from BNA Communications.
Five films dramatize EEO incidents that actually happened while accompanying manuals reinforce and expand on points made in the film. The "Primer of Equal Employment Opportunity" gives an overview of the regulations. Together they enable managers and supervisors to explore the basic premises of the regulations and find out how these regulations can work for them.
Visual Units (Films or videocassettes):
  1. Recruitment, Selection, and Placement
  2. Promotion and Transfer
  3. Discipline and Discharge
  4. Preventing Sexual Harassment
  5. Preventing Age Discrimination

Sexual Harassment Awareness Program.
Xerox Learning Systems, 1600 Summer Street, P.O. Box 10211, Stamford, CT 06904.
This program consists of a two-hour, small-group workshop that depicts both male and female points of view, and complete administrator and participant materials for easy facilitation. Objectives are to create an awareness of sexual harassment, its consequences, and individual-managerial roles and responsibilities.

Tell Someone: A Program for Combatting Sexual Harassment.
Affirmative Action Office, University of Michigan, 5080 Fleming Administration Building, Ann Arbor, MI 48109.

This training program includes videotape segments for faculty and students with a trainer's manual, pamphlets, and posters.

You Are the Game.
Office of Women's Affairs, Indiana University, Memorial Hall East 123, Bloomington, IN 47405.

An educational package for use with faculty, staff, and students, this program includes a videotaped dramatization of two sexual harassment incidents, a discussion guide, and results of a nationwide survey of institutions and their perceptions and guidelines for sexual harassment cases (for rent or purchase).

In Case of Sexual Harassment: A Guide for Women Students.
Project on the Status and Education of Women Association of American Colleges, 1818 R St. NW, Washington, DC 20009.

Filled with practical tips and sensible advice on issues such as: what is sexual harassment; who is likely to be harassed; what you can do and should not do about it; formal and informal institutional ways to deal with it; myths and facts about sexual harassment; risks involved in dating your professor; and a selected list of resources.

Appendices

A. University Policies
    and Informational Materials

B. A Model Policy for Field Settings

C. Educational and Training Materials

Appendix A
University Policies and
Informational Materials

F ollowing are several sexual harassment policies and other materials that present sound approaches to dealing with sexual harassment on campus. The methods used in the complaint and grievance processes of the university policies vary, and readers may want to assess the appropriateness of each policy for their own setting. The information from brochures and other university publications can be selected and arranged to address the needs of each academic setting effectively.

University of St. Thomas
Sexual Harassment Policy

The University of St. Thomas believes strongly in the human dignity of each individual. Therefore, the university strongly condemns and opposes any behavior on the part of any of the members of its community which constitutes sexual harassment.

Sexual harassment includes unwelcome sexual advances, requests for sexual favors, sexually motivated physical conduct, or other verbal or physical conduct or communication of a sexual nature when:

1. submission to that conduct or communication is made a term or condition, either explicitly or implicitly, of obtaining employment or education;
2. submission to or rejection of that conduct or communication by an individual is used as a factor in decisions affecting that individual's employment or education;
3. that conduct or communication has the purpose or effect of substantially interfering with an individual's employment or education, or creating an intimidating, hostile, or offensive employment or educational environment.

It is especially the case that the use of a position of authority to seek to accomplish any of the above constitutes sexual harassment.

Such unacceptable conduct might include but is not limited to:

1. repeated offensive sexual flirtations, unwelcome advances, propositions, or invitations;
2. unwelcome repeated comments, displays, or suggestions of a sexual nature which are individual or gender oriented;
3. objectionable physical contact, including touching.

Resolution of Situations

When a sexual harassment situation occurs, the victim should, if comfortable in doing so, clearly and straightforwardly object to the offender, pointing out the nature of the offense and indicating that the offender should not repeat the objectionable behavior.

All incidents of sexual harassment should be reported to the proper authority as soon as possible. The victim, if not comfortable in discussing the matter with the offender, should still report the incident.

If the victim is a:

1. Faculty member, contact Dr. Ralph Pearson, the Vice President for Academic Affairs (Telephone # 962-6720) or Dr. Miriam Williams, the Associate Vice President for Academic Affairs (Telephone # 962-6032)
2. Staff member, contact Ms. Patricia Taylor, the Director of Human Resources (Telephone # 962-6510) or Mr. Gerald Anderley, the Assistant Vice President for Facilities (Telephone # 962-6530)
3. Student, contact Mr. William Malevich, the Dean of Students (Telephone # 962-6050) or Ms. Barbara Shank, the Chair of the Social Work Department (Telephone # 962-5801)

The above designated administrators will promptly investigate complaints and report in writing the results of the investigation to the parties involved. All such complaints will be handled as discreetly as possible. If the complaint is found to have merit, prompt corrective or disciplinary action, up to and including dismissal from the University of St. Thomas, will be taken. Retaliatory action, if any, on the part of the offender will also result in corrective disciplinary action. Reports from the designated administrator on each sexual harassment complaint and resolution thereof will be sent in writing to the Provost of the university.

Either party, the victim or the accused, may appeal the decision rendered by the above described administrator within five work days of receipt of the administrator's written decision. An appeal can be initiated by submitting a written statement to the Provost, explaining the basis for the appeal.

A hearing panel of three members, selected by the Provost from a pool comprised of members of the university community, shall hear the case and accept evidence, testimony, and argument concerning the alleged sexual harassment. The hearing panel shall make a written recommendation to the Provost which will: (1) affirm the original decision and sanction, (2) affirm the original decision and reduce or increase the original sanction, or (3) reverse the original decision. The Provost shall make the final decision, including the sanction to be applied.

The pool from which the three-member hearing panel will be selected will be comprised of students, faculty members and staff employees, each of whom will serve a two-year term. The university will provide the hearing pool with relevant training and education to assist them in the consideration of sexual harassment cases. The composition of the particular pool and the particular hearing panels will be within the complete discretion of the Provost.

Each hearing panel, in consultation with the Provost, will determine the procedures to be followed during the hearing. Procedural and other rights granted to either party pursuant to the faculty handbook, student handbook or other applicable handbook apply to the hearing process.

STUDENTS OR EMPLOYEES WHO ARE SUBJECT TO HARASSMENT ARE URGED TO USE THIS PROCESS TO RESOLVE PROBLEMS OF SEXUAL HARASSMENT.

This process is the university's recommended policy for investigating claims of sexual harassment and is in place to facilitate the filing of sexual harassment grievances. However, the university must investigate any complaint of sexual harassment of which it is aware. Additionally, the university may investigate complaints of sexual harassment in any way that it deems appropriate, regardless of whether such investigation complies with this policy.

San Francisco State University
Sexual Harassment Policy and Procedures
(August 1989)

The following University Executive Directive (85-09) is based on Chancellor's Office Executive Order 342 and was approved by the President on August 14, 1985.

Rights, Duties, and Responsibilities of the Faculty

Preamble. This policy provides a definition of sexual harassment. It specifies pre-disciplinary, pre-grievance procedures for reporting and resolving complaints of sexual harassment and recommends that an education program be initiated. Formal disciplinary and grievance procedures are already defined by existing policies, executive orders, codes, and collective bargaining contracts pertinent to University employees and students.[1]

No individual shall be subject to reprisal for using this policy, nor shall its use preclude subsequent disciplinary or grievance measures. All units of the campus community are expected to comply with this policy.

Except as needed in processing the complaint, both the Sexual Harassment Advisors and Sexual Harassment Officers are required to maintain confidentiality in dealing with sexual harassment complaints.

Definition of Sexual Harassment. Sexual Harassment is one person's use of University authority, rank, or position to distort a University relationship by conduct which emphasizes another person's sexuality. Sexual advances, requests for sexual favors, and other verbal or physical conduct of a sexual nature are forms of sexual harassment when the person with authority, rank, or position:

a. Requires submission as an explicit or implicit condition of instruction, employment, or participation in any University activity; or

---

[1] If the physical safety of any University individual is in question, the President will act immediately, within the authority of Title 5, Section 41301; the Education Code, Section 22505; or the Penal Code, Section 626.4 to protect the threatened party. Formal proceedings may be initiated immediately by the President in consultation with the Sexual Harassment Officer(s), and the appropriate grievance/disciplinary action officer.

b. Distorts academic or personnel evaluations based on response to such conduct; or

c. Hinders performance by creating or allowing sexually intimidating, hostile, or offensive behavior to occur in the University or in a University-related setting.

Sexual harassment is unethical, unprofessional, illegal, and against San Francisco State University policy. It may occur in written, spoken, physical, and visual forms. The University will act to eliminate sexual harassment within its jurisdiction. A person with University authority, rank, or position must not use that power to create sexual pressure on someone else or on the workplace in general.

The University will evaluate each incident of alleged sexual harassment and apply appropriate remedies.

The University can dismiss employees or expel students for sexual harassment.

The University recognizes that any member of the campus community might be called upon to listen to a complaint of alleged sexual harassment. The listener should be objective and attentive, while discouraging use of names. No records should be kept, nor should promises for specific action or final decisions be made. The listener should refer the complainant to a Sexual Harassment Advisor or to a University Sexual Harassment Officer. Complainants may go to the Sexual Harassment Officer without first consulting a Sexual Harassment Advisor and may request an investigation at any time.

Sexual Harassment Advisors (SHA). All SHAs are volunteers. The Sexual Harassment Officers shall arrange for a course for training of advisors. People who have successfully completed the course may serve as SHAs. Advisors will be available to serve as sources of initial information to any individual who has a complaint or who needs information about sexual harassment.

The names of the advisors shall be published at the beginning of each semester. Advisors will have information about applicable laws, University policies and procedures, and options available for resolution of complaints. The Advisors shall:

a. Serve as resource persons to individuals with complaints or inquiries which may involve sexual harassment;

b. Advise the complainant regarding applicable University policies and procedures, and outline various informal and formal options;

c. Inform the appropriate sexual harassment officer if a complaint is received which is deemed sufficiently serious to warrant further action.

Discussion between complainants and Sexual Harassment Advisors shall occur without a written complaint and without identification of the person bringing the complaint and shall not imply guilt or innocence. No written record of specific complaints or actions taken to this point in the procedures shall be kept. However, a simple tally of the number and type of complaints shall be kept and reported to the appropriate Sexual Harassment Officer at the end of each semester.

If further action is requested by the complainant, the SHA shall refer the complainant to a Sexual Harassment Officer (SHO) and explain the responsibilities and duties of those officers. In addition, SHAs have an obligation to notify SHOs when it appears the University should act, even if the complainant has not requested further action. The SHA is not authorized to notify either the accused or any supervisor of the accused.

Sexual Harassment Officers (SHO). Sexual Harassment Officers are presidential designees and in that capacity are accountable directly to the President. The SHOs shall be the Director of Personnel or designee, Associate Dean for Faculty Affairs, and Associate Dean of Students. SHOs are empowered to hear and evaluate each complaint of alleged sexual harassment and to attempt resolution. SHOs shall observe basic standards of due process and confidentiality in all actions.

The Sexual Harassment Officers shall pursue complaints promptly through the stages outlined below.

Any discussion, investigation, or action taken under these procedures shall not conflict with student grievance procedures, regulations governing student affairs, collective bargaining contracts, and Executive Order 419.

Pre-Formal Resolution of Complaints. The complainant may choose to enter into a pre-formal discussion or to request that the SHO conduct an investigation immediately (see "Pre-Formal Investigation and Reporting" below).

Pre-Formal Discussion. Pre-formal discussion or resolution does not require a written complaint. Any SHO will hear complaints, determine the remedy sought, and review options for resolution. The review shall include a discussion of applicable University policies and procedures as well as external options for resolution. The SHO(s) shall aid the complainant in identifying ways in which further harassment might be prevented. University policy requires that the SHO keep written records of all complaints. Such records need not identify complainant or alleged harasser by name, nor shall they be part of any individual's official file at this stage of the procedure.

At the request of the complainant, the SHO(s) may attempt to resolve the situation by taking some or all of the following steps:

a. Informing the alleged harasser directly or through an appropriate administrator or supervisor that a problem has been raised concerning that person's conduct.

b. Informing the alleged harasser of University policy regarding sexual harassment.

c. Assisting the alleged harasser in identifying behavior which might lead to complaints and ways in which that behavior might be changed to avoid further complaints.

d. Recommending that an oral or written warning or reprimand be issued to the alleged harasser.

Pre-Formal Investigation and Reporting. At the request of the complainant and upon receipt of a written and signed complaint, the appropriate SHO shall initiate an investigation. If the SHO determines that circumstances so warrant, the SHO shall initiate an investigation with or without the consent of the complainant. The SHO shall notify the President, all the appropriate grievance/disciplinary officers for faculty or staff or students, and the alleged harasser that an investigation is underway, and give the names of the parties involved.

The appropriate SHO shall conduct a full and impartial investigation. The investigation procedures may include a meeting(s) at which both the complainant and the alleged harasser are present. If such a meeting(s) results in a settlement, the terms of the settlement shall be put in writing and be signed by the complainant, the alleged harasser, and the SHO.

At the conclusion of the investigation or upon settlement, the appropriate SHO shall submit a written report to the President. The report shall include a description of the facts, the remedy sought by the complainant or the terms of the signed settlement, and recommendations for further action if deemed necessary by the SHO. These recommendations shall be based upon the strength of evidence against the accused, the seriousness of action(s) that led to the complaint, and the remedy sought by the complainant. If formal disciplinary action is initiated, copies of the report shall be sent to the appropriate grievance/disciplinary action officer for faculty or staff or students, as well as the complainant and the accused.

Upon receipt of the SHO's report, the President or grievance/disciplinary action officer shall:

a. Make every attempt to resolve the complaint to the satisfaction of both complainant and the accused;

b. Inform both parties of procedures available to them should either be dissatisfied with the resolution of the complaint.

If either party is dissatisfied with actions taken up to this point, she/he may seek redress through existing complaint, grievance, or disciplinary procedures in student policies, codes, or contracts applicable to the bargaining unit or employment category to which the alleged harasser belongs.

Should it become necessary to invoke formal reprimand or disciplinary procedures, sexual harassment will be viewed as unprofessional conduct.

Formal disciplinary procedures will be pursued by the appropriate grievance/disciplinary action officer.

Sexual Harassment Complaint Process. The complainant may go directly to a Sexual Harassment Advisor (SHA) or to a Sexual Harassment Officer (SHO) or both and may request any one of the paths be taken, including immediate formal investigation.

Educational Program. A University program should be offered which defines the nature of sexual harassment, its negative psychological effects, its destructive impact on productivity, and its potential costs in the event of litigation. The availability of such a program should be appropriately publicized within the University community and also to the general public.

Campus resource materials for implementing an individual, self-study education program should be made available through the SHOs and the campus library.

Table 1. Sexual Harassment Complaint Process—
San Francisco State University

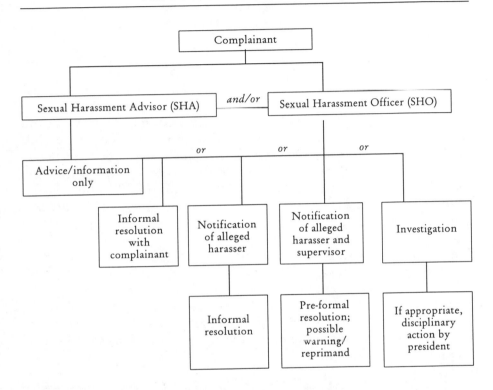

University of Washington
School of Social Work
(August 2, 1991)

Dear Students:

The School of Social Work is an academic community dedicated to the ideals of social justice. Its faculty, staff, and students aim not just to espouse social justice, but also to practice it in our daily interaction. As part of that commitment, we are working to ensure that the school is an environment in which discriminatory and harassing behavior, including inappropriate use of authority, does not occur to any person or property based upon race, color, religion, gender, sexual orientation, disability, or national origin. We must work together to create a safe environment for all members of our diverse school community.

Unfortunately, despite this commitment, instances of harassing or discriminatory behavior do occasionally occur. Procedures exist within the school and university for preventing and eliminating such behavior. If at any point you feel that you experienced harassment because of your race, gender, ethnic background, disability, or sexual orientation, you have the choice to take several actions to stop such behavior. These include:

1. **Informal Complaint Procedures**
   You may discuss the issues with one of the deans, the school of social work ombudsman, or the appropriate supervisor or faculty member. When possible, it is desirable to try to resolve such matters at the lowest possible level, but we do recognize that you must feel comfortable with the level and procedure used. When you discuss a complaint with any of the above individuals, you can expect confidentiality. If, however, your complaint is about sexual harassment, then the dean, the school ombudsman, or the appropriate supervisor or faculty member is legally obligated to report your complaint to the Ombudsman for Sexual Harassment or to the Human Rights Office. You, however, still have the right to decide whether or not you want to take the next step and speak with either of those representatives.

   If resolution of the complaint cannot be reached through your discussion with one of the deans, the school ombudsman or the appropriate supervisor or faculty member, then you may take another step in the informal complaint procedure by consulting informally with staff of the Human Rights Office (telephone 543-2717) or the university ombudsman/ombudsman for Sexual Harassment (Lois Price Spratlen, 543-0283). Additional information about sexual harassment, its procedures and how to prevent and stop it are printed in the student's program manual.

2. **Formal Complaint Procedures**
   When the complaint cannot be resolved informally, you may want to pursue more formal procedures. A formal complaint must be reported within six months of the most recent alleged discriminatory act. In cases of sexual harassment, reports are to be made to the ombudsman for sexual harassment (if the complaint is in regard to the actions of a faculty member, or a teaching or research assistant) or to the Human Rights Office (if the complaint is in regard to the actions of a staff member). The decision to make either a formal or informal complaint about harassment of any kind is the choice of the student. The procedures explained above are in place because it is your right to be protected from harassment.

While it is the responsibility of all of us to implement the ideals of social justice within the school, the Dean's Office is strongly committed to developing and implementing the procedures necessary for each member of our school community to enjoy a safe and supportive environment. Please do not hesitate to contact the Dean's Office if you have questions about any of these procedures.

Sincerely,

Nancy R. Hooyman
Dean

University of Washington
Policy Prohibiting Sexual Harassment

The university is committed to the principle that the campus environment must be free from all forms of discrimination, including sexual harassment. Sexual harassment is defined in university policy as follows:

> Sex discrimination in the form of sexual harassment, defined as the use of one's authority or power, either explicitly or implicitly, to coerce another into unwanted sexual relations or to punish another for his/her refusal, or as the creation by a member of the university community of an intimidating, hostile or offensive working or educational environment through verbal or physical conduct of a sexual nature, shall be a violation of the university's human rights policy. (UW Handbook, Vol. 4, p. 44)

Sexual harassment on campus occurs when a faculty member makes demands or requests from students for sexual favors in exchange for grades or academic progress, or punishes a student for refusing such sexual advances. Similarly, it is sexual harassment when supervisory staff or faculty demand sexual favors in exchange for employment or promotional opportunities. Unwelcome comments of a sexual nature, repeated touchings, or approaches to students and staff create an offensive working and educational environment, and are also incidents of sexual harassment. Such conduct towards patients and all campus visitors is equally offensive. Sexual harassment violates federal and state law as well as university rules and regulations, and will subject the offender to serious university action and potential personal liability.

The university has implemented an active program of campus education to inform the university community about the definition of and strictures against sexual harassment, as well as to identify the university resources that are available to assist persons who encounter such conduct. While the goal of the university is to prevent inappropriate practices through education, the university vigorously enforces its prohibitions against these behaviors and rigorously follows its internal processes to investigate and remedy violations.

You should discuss any concerns you have about sexual harassment with your department chair, area personnel representative, or direct supervisor. Also, the following university officials are available to discuss with you instances of sexual harassment, on a confidential basis if requested, or to advise you on university procedures.

Faculty and Students
Dr. Lois Price Spratlen
University Ombudsman and
  Ombudsman for Sexual
  Harassment
301 Student Union
543-0283 or 543-6028

Professional, Classified
  and Student Employees
Dr. Helen Remick
  Assistant Provost
Frank Trevino, Jr., Director
Human Rights Office
4045 Brooklyn Avenue N.E.
543-1830 or 543-7217

The university is committed to protecting the rights and dignity of each individual in the university community.

Office of the President
October 1988

University of Washington

STOP SEXUAL HARASSMENT

Sexual Harassment is Illegal

Because sexual harassment is a type of sex discrimination, you may also file a formal complaint of sex discrimination with:

- The Human Rights Office
- The Equal Employment Officer
- Washington State Human Opportunity Commission
- U.S. Equal Employment Opportunity Commission
- U.S. Office for Civil Rights, Department of Education

UW Provides a System to Help You, But We Can Act Only If You Tell

While most harassment involves men harassing women, either men or women can be harassed by members of the same or opposite sex. The University of Washington policy prohibits all forms of sexual harassment.

The University will carry out a thorough investigation in formal complaint situations to protect the rights of both the person complaining and the alleged harasser. The University has been very successful in resolving both formal and informal complaints.

University of Washington Policy on Sexual Harassment

Sex discrimination in the form of sexual harassment, defined as the use of one's authority or power, either explicitly or implicitly, to coerce another into unwanted sexual relations or to punish another for his or her refusal, or as the creation by a member of the University community of an intimidating, hostile or offensive working or educational environment through verbal or physical conduct of a sexual nature, shall be a violation of the University's human rights policy.

University Handbook
Vol. 4, p. 44

University of Washington
Examples of Sexual Harassment

Beth's professor has just approved her course selection for her third year of graduate study. As she leaves, he tells her that if he got to know her personally outside the classroom he could help her with her job search. He then reaches out and gives her a squeeze. Upset about what just happened, Beth talks about it with other students in the program and discovers that the same professor had recently made similar suggestions to two others. They decide to report him to the Dean. The Dean reprimands the professor and warns him that if such behavior occurs in the future he will be relieved of his graduate advising responsibilities.

Connie hears her first discussion of sexual harassment as part of a staff training session. She realizes then that when her supervisor clips sexually suggestive notes to her assignments, such as "I work better after hours, let's talk about this over drinks" or "How about discussing this at my place tonight?," it constitutes sexual harassment. Connie sees that she has needlessly tolerated this behavior hoping that it would go away. It hasn't. She decides to report these incidents to the Human Rights Investigator and discuss what action she could take in the future.

Jennifer's major professor is going through a divorce. Lately while talking about her dissertation, he has begun telling her about his fantasies and pressuring her into making his fantasies come true. She has refused, but now he is saying that she will never finish her dissertation if she doesn't have sex with him. Jennifer is extremely depressed and fearful that her career is at stake. She is considering dropping out of the program.

Sexual Harassment Includes Any Unwanted Sexual Attention, Such As:

- sexually suggestive looks or gestures
- sexual teasing or jokes
- pressure for dates
- deliberate touching, cornering, pinching
- attempts to kiss or fondle
- pressure for sex
- requests for sex in exchange for grades, promotions, or salary increases

Help Is Available

If you believe you are being harassed, seek help—the earlier the better.

The University of Washington has designated special people to help you. They are:

- University Ombudsman and Ombudsman for Sexual Harassment (for complaints against faculty members & teaching assistants) Lois Price Spratlen, 301 Student Union 543-6028
- Human Rights Office (all other complaints) 4045 Brooklyn Avenue NE, Room 126 543-7217

You can speak to them confidentially. After discussing your case, they can provide you with options on how to deal with the harassment. These options range from suggestions on how to discourage the harasser yourself to filing a formal complaint. The Ombudsman or Human Rights Investigator may speak formally with the harasser and his or her supervisor in an effort to correct the situation and to prevent retaliation.

Are you afraid that:

- you will suffer retaliation from the harasser?
- people will think "you asked for it"?
- you have misread the initiator's intentions?
- you are somehow responsible for the harasser's behavior?

These fears are often reported by people who have suffered from unwanted sexual advances. *You are not alone.* Don't accept these actions as the "way things are." You do not have to endure abuse from people in positions of power.

You Can Take Action

SAY NO. Tell the harasser that his or her advances are unwanted and you want them stopped.

DON'T DELAY. Pay attention to cues or comments indicating harassment. If a person's behavior makes you uncomfortable, say so.

KEEP A RECORD. Should the harassment continue, keep track of dates, times, places, and statements. This information can be used to support a complaint.

TALK TO OTHERS. Let the department chair, supervisor of the harasser, your personnel representative, or the ombudsman know what has happened. Check with other students or co-workers to see whether they also have been harassed; incidents of harassment are often not isolated, and sexual harassers are likely to exhibit a pattern of such behavior. Tell one of the University administrators responsible for dealing with sexual harassment.

The University of North Carolina at Chapel Hill
Allied . . . for a Safe Campus Community

A number of programs and services have been developed to provide the UNC-Chapel Hill community with the very best in support services, campus safety, and education regarding sexual assault and harassment. Two groups have formed to meet the needs of this campus and they have developed a comprehensive approach to dealing with the issues of rape and sexual harassment. In addition, numerous satellite programs are in existence and are closely aligned with the overall project. A brief description of what we offer follows:

Rape Action Project (966-4041)

At the center of our program is the Rape Action Project, a student-run organization focusing on sexual assault and harassment issues. It consists of interested students who meet regularly to discuss their various projects and to plan events with contributing campus departments and local agencies. Founded spring 1986, it is a recognized student group that receives funding through the Student Congress with student activities fees. A staff member from the Dean of Students Office serves as advisor to the group. Supplementary funding is provided through the Student Affairs Division.

One of the most important projects this group offers is its peer-presentations on date/acquaintance rape and sexual harassment. Teams of trained students present a 60-minute film and/or discussion for a variety of on and off-campus groups.

Over the years, some of the Rape Action Project activities have included a campus security survey, Rape Awareness Weeks, orientation presentations, promotion of campus support services for victims of sexual assault, identifying funds for overnight charges for victims at the Student Health Services infirmary ("Student Stay Fund"), and adapting the Student Judicial Code to include specific wording regarding sexual assault and sexual harassment.

As of fall 1989, the RAP has existed as the product of a merger with students from the Sexual Harassment Task Force, which formed in spring 1989 to deal with campus harassment issues. In line with this merger, the current RAP presenters are trained in both sexual assault and sexual harassment, preparing them to meet the student community's needs in both areas.

Rape Awareness Committee

Serving as a resource group for student organizations is the Rape Awareness Committee, which is comprised of representatives from the following departments or agencies:

Dean of Students Office
Student Psychological Services
GYN Clinic/Student Health Serv.
Student Health Education
University Police
University Counseling Center
Faculty
Campus Ministries
Student Judicial Program

UNC Housing
Orange Co. Rape Crisis Center
Chapel Hill Police Depart.
Coalition for Battered Women
Greek Councils
Rape Action Project (student)
SAFE Escort (student)
Student Government (student)
Daily Tar Heel (student)
Media Contacts:
    Chapel Hill Newspaper
    Chapel Hill Herald

This group, facilitated by a member of the Office of the Dean of Students, meets monthly. Members report on the rape-related activities of their particular departments or agency. In addition, they serve as valuable resources for the needs identified by the student groups. These meetings have been most productive in cutting down on duplication of efforts, making the best use of our resources and helping to publicize the many fine services and programs offered to our community. This group is responsible for assisting in the development and implementation of educational programs on sexual assault/harassment for freshman orientation and UNC housing staff. In addition, the Rape Awareness Committee oversees functioning of the University's Sexual Assault Response Plan, including annual review of and training for implementation of the Plan.

Students Averting Frightening Encounters (SAFE) Escort (962-SAFE)

This student-sponsored escort service is designed to promote safety on campus. SAFE currently operates both campus-wide and library-based services. This valuable resource functions primarily on weeknights with some limited weekend hours.

University Police (966-3230)

This department offers a presentation entitled "Dealing with Rape" and focuses on the larger issues of campus violence and safety tips.

Student Health Education (966-6586)
Student Psychological Services (966-3658)
University Counseling Center (962-2175)

A number of additional programs are available through various departments within the Student Health Division and the Division of Student Affairs. Student Health Education provides information on such topics as surviving a sexual assault and male/female relationships. Student Psychological Services provides the campus community with individual counseling and support groups for women who have had unwanted sexual experiences. In addition, the University Counseling Center also serves as a resource for individual counseling and information for victims of sexual assault and harassment.

Orange County Rape Crisis Center
(Hotline: 967-7273, Office: 968-4647)

This local agency provides a valuable resource to the campus community in offering a variety of sexual assault and safety programs to our students as well as support services and counseling referrals. In addition, the center offers support groups for sexual assault victims and adult survivors of child sexual abuse.

Appendix B
A Model Policy for Field Settings

A s research in the Valentine et al. article demonstrates, typical university policies regarding sexual harassment on campus may not be sufficient to cover the special risks that social work students face in field placement agencies. The policy created by the University of South Carolina has been developed specifically to cover those situations. Administrators and faculty should review this policy as a model policy and consider what additions or amendments may be needed in their own settings.

University of South Carolina
Sexual Harassment in the Field Setting

It is the policy of the University of South Carolina College of Social Work, in order to maintain an environment in which the dignity and worth of all students are respected, that sexual harassment of students in their field placements is intolerable and unacceptable. It is a form of behavior that seriously undermines the atmosphere of trust essential to the learning environment. This policy is in keeping with Federal and State laws prohibiting sex discrimination. It is also the policy of the University that willful false accusations of sexual harassment will not be condoned.

The College of Social Work recognizes that, in many instances, the sexual harassment policies and procedures adopted by the University of South Carolina may not apply to the sexual harassment of a field student in an agency where he/she is not an employee of the agency or where harassment is coming from someone who is not a University instructor. It is important that there be guidelines that pertain to complaints regarding sexual harassment of students because of the unavoidable subordinate position students experience in field placement settings. Sexual harassment of interns can be destructive to the learning environment, demoralizing to the student and adversely affect his/her performance in the agency. Sexual harassment of student interns may include harassment from a field instructor or an agency employee.

A. Definition
  1. Sexual harassment may involve the behavior of the field instructor or any person employed by the field agency of either sex when such behavior falls within the definition outlined below.
  2. Sexual harassment of a student from the University of South Carolina is defined as unwelcome sexual advances, requests for sexual favors, verbal or other expressive behaviors, or physical conduct commonly understood to be of a sexual nature when:
     a. submission to such conduct is made either explicitly or implicitly a term or condition of an individual's continued placement;
     b. submission to or rejection of such conduct is used as a basis for decisions or assessments affecting the individual's welfare as a student placed in the agency;

c. such conduct has the purpose or effect of unreasonably and substantially interfering with an individual's welfare, academic, or professional performance, or creates an intimidating, hostile, offensive, and demeaning work or educational environment.

Examples of Prohibited Behavior

Prohibited acts of sexual harassment may take a variety of forms ranging from subtle pressure for sexual activity to physical assault. Examples of the kinds of conduct included in the definition of sexual harassment include, but are not limited to:
1. threats or intimidation of sexual relations or sexual contact which is not freely or mutually agreeable to both parties;
2. continual or repeated verbal abuses of a sexual nature including graphic commentaries about a person's body, sexually degrading words to describe the person, or propositions of a sexual nature;
3. threats or insinuations that the person's employment, grades, wages, promotional opportunities, classroom or work assignments, or other conditions of continued placement may be adversely affected by not submitting to sexual advances.

Consensual Relationships

Consensual sexual relationships between field instructor and student, or between student and an agency employee, while not expressly forbidden, are generally deemed unwise. Such relationships, though they may be appropriate in other settings, are inappropriate when they occur between members of the teaching staff and students. A professional power differential exists in these situations in terms of the influence and authority which the one can exercise over the other. If a charge of sexual harassment is lodged regarding a once-consenting relationship, the burden may be on the alleged offender to prove that the sexual harassment policy was not violated.

B. Field Agency Approval

Sexual harassment of any student intern from the College of Social Work shall not be tolerated from any field instructor, employee, or representative of the field agency. To best ensure that students are placed in an agency environment free from sexual harassment the following will occur:
1. Each field agency and field instructor shall receive a copy of the College of Social Work's Sexual Harassment in the Field Setting Policy.

2. Any agency or field setting approved for use as a field placement should provide the Field Committee with a Sexual Harassment Policy which shall be kept on file. If the agency has
no such policy, the College of Social Work strongly urges that
one be developed.

C. Procedures

When a student believes that he/she has been the subject of sexual
harassment in the field agency setting, the student will notify his/
her field instructor and field liaison. The student may also wish
to discuss the issue with his/her advisor or a College of Social
Work faculty member. If the sexual harassment involved the
student's agency instructor, the student may notify the field
instructor's supervisor. If the agency has a specifically designated
individual or office to deal with these matters, that person or
office would also be notified by the student. The student would
be strongly encouraged to notify agency personnel. If the student
prefers, the College of Social Work will notify the appropriate
agency personnel.

The College faculty member receiving the report shall immediately notify the Dean of the College of Social Work, who with the
faculty liaison and the Director of Field will investigate the
complaint.

The investigation may include the following:

1. A meeting with the student making the complaint. The student
may be accompanied by another support person. At this time,
the student is encouraged to submit a written statement regarding the nature of the harassment. This statement should be as
specific as possible including date(s) and time(s) and individual(s)
involved. If the student made any attempt to confront the
situation, this should also be included in the written report.
2. A meeting with the Field Instructor and other relevant agency
personnel.
3. A meeting with the alleged violator.
4. A review of the agency's sexual harassment policy.

**Because sexual harassment is not an interpersonal issue nor is
the investigation a legal proceeding, a group meeting requiring
the student to confront the alleged violator will not be required.**

Based on the investigation, the Dean shall determine if the
agency policy on sexual harassment has been followed and if the
student is safe and will be free from further harassment. The resolution of the investigation may include but is not limited to the
following:

1. The complaint was founded and satisfactorily addressed by the field agency and the student should remain in the field placement.
2. The complaint was founded and satisfactorily addressed by the field agency but the student should be placed in an alternate field placement.
3. The complaint was founded and not satisfactorily addressed by the field agency and the student should be placed in another field placement.
4. The complaint was founded and not satisfactorily addressed and the agency should not be approved as a field placement setting.
5. The complaint was unfounded and the student should remain in the placement.
6. The complaint was unfounded and the student should be placed in an alternate field placement.

Students following these procedures are in no way inhibited from pursuing other options such as bringing the matter to the attention of the College of Social Work Grievance Committee, the University of South Carolina/Senior Vice President for Student Affairs or the System Affirmative/Action Officer, or pursuing legal channels. No student intern will be subject to restraint, interference, coercion, or reprisal for seeking information about sexual harassment, filing a sexual harassment complaint or serving as a witness.

Passed by College of Social
Work Faculty: 10/17/90

Appendix C
Educational and Training Materials

T he following educational and training materials were prepared at the College of St. Catherine/University of St. Thomas and the University of Washington Schools of Social Work. The materials are provided to assist schools and departments of social work in developing their own training materials in sexual harassment and other forms of discriminatory behaviors. Please feel free to use and adapt these materials for your own school.

1. Basic Information on Sexual Harassment
    College of St. Catherine/University of St. Thomas

2. Training Outline and Materials
    College of St. Catherine/University of St. Thomas
    School of Social Work

3. Posters/Discussion Materials
    University of Washington School of Social Work

Basic Information on Sexual Harassment

College of St. Catherine/University of St. Thomas

Statutory Bases for Sexual Harassment

A. Title VII of the Civil Rights Act of 1964
B. Title IX of the Higher Education Amendment
C. State Human Rights Act
D. City Ordinances

Sexual Harassment Defined

1. Unwelcome sexual advances;
2. Requests for sexual favors;
3. Sexually motivated physical conduct; and
4. Other verbal or physical conduct of a sexual nature, when:
   a. submission to that conduct is made a term or condition of an individual's employment or education;
   b. submission to that conduct is used as a factor affecting an individual's employment or education;
   c. the conduct has the purpose or effect of substantially interfering with an individual's employment or education; or
   d. the conduct has the purpose or effect of creating an intimidating, hostile, or offensive employment or educational environment.

Two Types of Sexual Harassment

A. *Quid Pro Quo Harassment*—involves an employer's sexually discriminating behavior which compels an employee or student to choose between acceding to sexual demands or forfeiting job or educational benefits, continued employment or promotion, or otherwise suffering tangible job or educational detriments.

B. *Hostile Environment Harassment*—federal and state law prohibit sexual harassment that creates a "hostile work or educational environment." For such harassment to be actionable, it must be sufficiently severe or pervasive to unreasonably interfere with an individual's performance or create an "intimidating, hostile, or offensive environment."

Critical Factors in Determining Hostile Environment Sexual Harassment

Determining "Unwelcomeness"

1. Conduct must be unsolicited.
2. Perspective.
3. Whether the individual complained of the conduct to his/her supervisor or other proper authority.
4. The victim's own behavior.
5. "Unwelcome" does not necessarily mean "involuntary."

Elements of Sexual Harassment

1. Sexual harassment is a process and not an event.
2. Sexual harassment is a violation of intimacy barriers/roles/boundary issues in the employer-employee, teacher-student, field instructor-student relationship.
3. Sexual harassment takes place in professional, social, religious, and educational environments.
4. Sexual harassment has an adverse impact on the victim, the harasser, the institution/organization and on society. The impact can be: economic, academic/job performance, emotional stress, physical stress, productivity, motivation/morale, dropout/job turnover, and/or legal costs.
5. Sexual harassment is illegal.
6. Sexual harassment is an abuse of power.
7. Sexual harassment disrupts the educational process.
8. Sexual harassment creates a discriminatory climate.
9. Sexual harassment reinforces institutional sexism.

What Can Be Done to Eliminate Sexual Harassment?

1. Develop a clear institutional policy prohibiting sexual harassment.
2. Conduct seminars, workshops and other educational programs to sensitize faculty, students and field instructors to sexual harassment issues.
3. Reassure students that they will not be penalized for reporting.
4. Publicize and enforce a consistent set of sanctions against sexual harassment.
5. Say "NO" to the harasser. Do not ignore the sexual advance in the hope that it will not be repeated. This does not work. Direct, assertive action by the victim is the most effective way in dealing with the problem. Most often, it will stop once the harasser realizes the conduct is unwelcome.
6. Keep notes on what happened. Talk to friends, co-workers or fellow students as a source of support.
7. Report the problem to the proper authority.

Training Outline and Training Materials

College of St. Catherine/University of St. Thomas

School of Social Work

Sexual Harassment Workshop Outline

- Workshop Objectives
- Questionnaire/Topics for Discussion
- Definitions of Sexual Harassment
- Statutory Bases
- Environmental Characteristics Contributing to Sexual Harassment
- Critical Incidents for Discussion
- Consenting Relationships
- Case Examples for Discussion
- What Can Be Done?
- How to Avoid Allegations of Sexual Harassment
- Administrative Procedures and Management Strategies to Prevent Sexual Harassment
- Personal Costs to the Victim
- Overview
- Discussion Questions
- Posters/Discussion Materials
- Handout on Peer Harassment
- Six Thing I've Always Wanted to Know About Harrassment, But Was Afraid to Ask

Workshop Objectives

1. To understand what sexual harassment is and what to do when it occurs.
2. To understand the issues around academic and workplace sexual harassment.
3. To discuss these issues using a systems perspective.
4. To review the continuum of challenge through violation of professional boundaries.
5. To review common harasser, victim, and organizational characteristics that increase the likelihood of sexual harassment.
6. To review administrative procedures and management strategies to prevent sexual harassment.
7. To become more aware and sensitive to the issue of sexual harassment.

Questionnaire/Topics for Discussion

Read the following and decide if each situation illustrated represents a potential case of sexual harassment.

Sexual Harassment?

1. Supervisor X jokes a lot in the office about women's sexuality; he teases some of the women staff about their sex lives or sexual preferences. Some staff think it's funny; others are embarrassed. Some of the women staff he teases have quit coming to work.
Yes   No   Unsure

2. Whenever Social Worker A goes in to see her supervisor with questions about her assignments, he seems more interested in talking about personal matters—his sex life and hers; the last time they met, he suggested they have their meeting over drinks at a nearby bar. If she could avoid supervision, she feels she'd rather work on her own and avoid the hassle.
Yes   No   Unsure

3. Over the year Social Worker B has firmly but politely declined a number of offers from Supervisor C to see him socially. Now at the end of the year, she is surprised to learn that her position as team coordinator is not being renewed for the coming year.
Yes   No   Unsure

4. Field instructor Ms. V is having trouble with Student W; he behaves in a disruptive manner and flouts her authority. Recently, Ms. V tried to talk to him about his behavior. He told her if she "got laid" more often she wouldn't find his behavior so objectionable. Later that evening, she received a series of obscene phone calls, which she believes were made by some of his friends.
Yes   No   Unsure

5. Every morning the agency director comes
in and hugs all the women in the office. He
says "I'm just a very affectionate person."   Yes   No   Unsure

6. Social Worker C's boss offers her a
promotion if she'll go out with him.
She accepts and as a result receives the
promotion she and two other women in
the agency were vying for.   Yes   No   Unsure

7. At a meeting of his professional staff
the agency director asks the only woman
present to serve the coffee.   Yes   No   Unsure

8. Social Worker D's boss asks her to join
him for a drink after work to discuss her
new job responsibilities.   Yes   No   Unsure

9. Social Worker E's co-worker John
remarks how pretty she looks today
in her new dress.   Yes   No   Unsure

Definitions of Sexual Harassment

The Equal Employment Opportunity Commission guidelines define sexual harassment as unwelcome sexual advances, requests for sexual favors, and other verbal or physical conduct of a sexual nature when:

1. submission to such conduct is made explicitly or implicitly a term or condition of an individual's employment or participation in a university-sponsored education program or activity;

2. submission to or rejection of such conduct by an individual is used as the basis for academic or employment decisions affecting that individual; or

3. such conduct has the purpose or effect of substantially interfering with an individual's academic or work performance or creating an intimidating, hostile, or offensive working or educational environment.

Sexual harassment is any unwanted attention of a sexual nature from someone in the classroom or workplace that creates discomfort with the job or academic performance. Examples of sexual harassment may include the following if such behavior is unwelcomed and not reciprocated.

Verbal	Nonverbal	Physical
Sexual innuendo	Suggestive or	Touching
Insults	insulting sounds	Patting
Pressure for sexual	Leering or	Pinching
activity	ogling	Brushing
Sexist remarks about	Whistling	Coerced sexual
a person's body, or	Obscene gestures	intercourse
sexual activities		Assault
Implied or verbal		
threats concerning		
one's job or grades		
Sexual Propositions		

Figure 1.

A Continuum of Sexually Harassing Behavior

Gender Harassment: General sexist statements and behavior that insult or degrade an individual and/or convey discriminatory attitudes.

Seductive Behavior: Unwelcome and inappropriate physical or verbal sexual advances.

Sexual Bribery: The use of promises, rewards, and other types of bribes to solicit sexual favors.

Sexual Coercion: The use of threats to force an individual into sexual activity.

Sexual Assault: Forced sexual relations or activities.

Adapted from: Paludi, M.A., & Barickman, R.B. (1991). *Academic and workplace sexual harassment* (p. 6). Albany, NY: State University of New York Press.

Quid Pro Quo Harassment: This involves an employer's sexually discriminating behavior which compels an employee or student to choose between acceding to sexual demands or forfeiting job or educational benefits, continued employment or promotion, or otherwise suffering tangible job or educational detriments.

Sexual Favoritism: Where employment opportunities or benefits are granted because of an individual's submission to the employer's sexual advances or requests for sexual favors, the employer may be held liable for unlawful sex discrimination against other persons who were qualified for but denied that employment opportunity or benefit.

Hostile Environment Harassment: Federal and state law prohibit sexual harassment that creates a "hostile work or educational environment." For such harassment to be actionable, it must be sufficiently severe or pervasive to unreasonably interfere with an individual's performance or create an "intimidating, hostile, or offensive environment."

Statutory Bases

Title VII Applied to Sexual Harassment

1. Sexual harassment is a form of discrimination which applies to race, color, sex, religion, or national origin.
2. Harassment on the basis of sex is a violation of Sec. 703 of Title VII.
3. In determining whether the alleged conduct constitutes sexual harassment, the determination will be made from the facts, on a case by case basis.
4. The employer is responsible for its acts and those of its agents and supervisory employees with respect to sexual harassment regardless of whether the acts complained of were authorized, forbidden, or whether the employer knew or should have known of their occurrence.
5. The employer must take prompt and appropriate corrective action when it knows or should have known of the discriminatory harassment.
6. An employer may be responsible for the acts of non-employees with respect to sexual harassment of employees.
7. The employer should take all steps necessary to prevent sexual harassment including affirmatively raising the subject, expressing strong disapproval, developing appropriate sanctions, informing employees of their right to raise the issue, and developing methods to sensitize all concerned.
8. The employer is liable for discrimination against those who were denied employment opportunities or benefit because of sexual harassment.

Title IX Applied to Sexual Harassment

1. Discrimination will be held to exist where a student, because of his or her sex, is subject to demands or conditions that are not imposed on members of the opposite sex.
2. The advance or comment must be offensive to a student.
3. Sexual harassment of a student must adversely affect the learning environment.
4. The harassment must be by someone under the control of the institution.
5. The institution must take prompt and appropriate remedial action when it knows or should know of the discriminatory harassment.

Environmental Characteristics Contributing to Sexual Harassment

Institutional Characteristics

- High professional autonomy, little "direct supervision"
- Sexually oriented physical environment
- Sexually exploitative culture
- Professor/boss is the expert/authority figure
- Geographically isolated
- Lack of support and affirmation
- Large power differential among associates
- Relatively closed organizational system with stable, tenured faculties, long-term employees, and few new members
- Discomfort in discussing professionally unethical behavior, especially sexually related behavior

Harasser Characteristics

- Is cult-like figure or guru who behaves out of the grandiose belief that s/he knows what is best for others
- Has poor collegial relationships with other faculty and staff in their department and in the organization
- Lacks professional involvement with colleagues or peers
- Has problems in personal relationships
- Lacks knowledge and professional identification
- Has difficulty establishing and negotiating appropriate boundaries
- Sees students and other staff in inappropriate settings and at inappropriate hours
- Uses poor judgment
- Seems psychotic, neurotic, or otherwise mentally ill

Critical Incidents for Discussion

1. A client has a leading role in a play and invites staff member to attend.
2. Staff member dresses differently for some clients than for others.
3. Staff member regularly touches or hugs clients.
4. Supervisor falls in love with supervisee.
5. Staff member falls in love with client.
6. Staff member sees clients alone at the agency in the evening or makes home call on Saturday.
7. Supervisor regularly tells jokes with sexual themes.
8. Staff member makes sexist comments that are demeaning to women.
9. Staff member makes sexist remarks about a client's clothing, body, or sexual activity.
10. Supervisor gives staff a quick kiss hello or goodbye.

Consenting Relationships

Most sexual harassment policies do not specifically forbid sexual relationships between individuals where a professional power differential exists; however, they actively discourage even apparently consenting sexual relationships between supervisor and employee or faculty and student.

This warning is implied: "A supervisor who enters into a sexual relationship with a staff member, or faculty member who enters a relationship with a student, should realize that if a charge of sexual harassment is subsequently lodged, it will be exceedingly difficult to prove immunity on grounds of mutual consent."

Relationships between a student or employee and an administrator, coach, advisor, faculty member, program director, counselor, or residential staff member who has supervisory responsibility for that student or employee are included in this category.

The telling characteristic of the relationship is *power*. The supervisor or faculty member has it and the student or employee does not. They are not equal partners and therefore "consent" is not possible.

Case Examples for Discussion

Case 1. Jill was recently laid off as a student research assistant for a large research project. She had been involved with her supervisor for several months, but broke off the relationship just before she got the layoff notice. She was told the layoff was due to budget cuts, but Jill helped assemble the budget and knows this was not the reason.

Case 2. Linda is one of three women employed by a mental health agency. She asked a question in group supervision but it was time to end before her supervisor could answer. When he said he'd talk to her after group, the other women laughed. The supervisor raised his eyebrows and made a joke. Linda felt humiliated and never got her question answered.

Case 3. Leslie was very impressed by the interest a well-known practitioner showed in her work. Because of his encouragement, she chose to specialize in his area of expertise. Later, when she realized that his interest had been only sexual, she was astonished and angry. She felt humiliated and foolish for having believed he respected her work. She has left the agency and wonders if she will ever return to the field.

Case 4. Sophomore Tanya depends on a part-time job to stay in school. One Saturday while she was alone with her boss, he put his arms around her and invited her to go home with him that night. She ran away from him and did not go back to work. Now she can't pay her bills.

Case 5. Connie, a newly hired social worker, was invited by her female supervisor to share a hotel room when they attended a professional conference where she was presenting a workshop. When Connie refused, the supervisor accused her of being immature, telling her she doubted that Connie could handle future professional development situations.

Case 6. On the first day of the job, the human resource director asked the new employees to turn in information about themselves. One of the questions asked was whether they like recreational sex.

Case 7. Judy is a newly hired child care worker in a residential treatment program. Several male staff members regularly leave pornographic pictures where she will find them. She dreads going to work and is finding it harder to keep herself motivated because of the situation.

Case 8. Students in fieldwork placement know that their instructor is in a sexual relationship with one of their classmates. Although the fieldwork instructor and the student try to be discreet about their relationship, the other field students notice the special attention their classmate receives. They feel their classmate has an unfair advantage and they resent it.

What Can Be Done?

- Say "No!" to the harasser. Direct, assertive action by the victim is the most effective way to deal with the problem. Most often, it will stop once the offender realizes the conduct is unwelcome.

- Do not ignore the sexual advance in the hope it will not be repeated. This doesn't work.

- Keep notes. Keep a calendar; write down what happened and when, and who was there.

- Talk to friends and co-workers or fellow students as a source of support.

- Find out if others have been harassed by this same person. If so, would they support a complaint?

- Write a letter to the offending person indicating that the behavior must stop.

- Report the sexual harassment incident.

- Develop a clear institutional policy prohibiting sexual harassment.

- Conduct seminars, workshops, and other educational programs to sensitize employees, faculty, students, and field instructors to sexual harassment issues.

- Reassure employees and students that they will not be penalized for reporting.

How to Avoid Allegations of Sexual Harassment

1. Recognize that anyone may be considered a harasser if their behavior towards another becomes unwanted, offensive, hostile, or creates an offensive and disruptive work environment.

2. Do not assume that your behavior is acceptable to everyone with whom you come into contact. Remember, regardless of your intent, you may be appropriately accused of harassment if you indulge in such actions as:
   • Making sexual comments about another's clothing or body
   • Telling sexual jokes; using sexual innuendoes
   • Touching, hugging, patting, kissing
   • Making repeated, unwanted overtures of a sexual nature
   • Displaying lewd or offensive pictures/objects
   • Using lewd or offensive gestures

3. If you are a supervisor, make sure your subordinates feel comfortable telling you when they are offended or harassed.

4. Be aware of how people respond to what you do or say. If an individual objects to your behavior toward them, listen and heed their objections.

Administrative Procedures and Management Strategies to Prevent Sexual Harassment

Administrative Procedures

- Develop a clear mission statement
- Enforce fair hiring practices
- Create an agency statement forbidding sexual harassment and sexual involvement with clients
- Promote open channels of communication and collegial feedback through:
  - Staff supervision/peer review
  - Staff development/education
  - Outside organizational consultant
- Serve as a role model for others
- Be fair, objective, and clear about your expectations with all employees

Preventive Strategies

- Recognize the problem and address it in an objective, understanding, and efficient manner.
  - Address concerns of all involved
  - Maintain confidentiality
- Understand that we all need to learn new ways of relating to one another.
  - Examine your own behavior and attitudes
  - Recognize behavior which may be accepted but demeans another individual and CHANGE THAT BEHAVIOR
- Respect the opinions, thoughts, and work of women in the workplace/academic community.
  - Involve women in decision-making processes
  - Listen to and address the concerns of women
- Understand that women do not ask to be sexually harassed nor do they think it is "just part of the job."
  - Learn more about sexual harassment and discuss its implications with others
  - Talk to women about their perspectives/experiences with sexual harassment and support their speaking out
- Discourage and condemn any type of behavior, language, and/or materials which are sexist or discriminatory.
  - Sexist Remarks
  - Pornography

Personal Costs to the Victim

- Negative emotional reactions
  Anger, shock
  Fear; feelings of powerlessness, anxiety, or frustration
  Shame, guilt, feeling dirty
- Physical reactions
  Symptoms of stress—headaches, gastrointestinal problems, fatigue
  Sleeping too much or too little
  Eating too much or too little
  Nightmares
- Psychological reactions
  Feelings of lack of control, phobias, anxiety attacks
  Feelings of incompetency, negative self-image
- Social reactions
  Changes in daily habits
  Quitting work, dropping out of school
  Inability to perform job or academic responsibilities
  Absenteeism, skipping class
  Lack of trust, social isolation
  Inability to meet new people, be involved in intimate relationships

Overview

Sexual harassment is:

- Illegal
  - Title VII of the Civil Rights Act (for employees)
  - Title IX of the Higher Education Amendment (for students)
- A violation of professional ethics
- An abuse of power
- Disruptive of the educational process
- Encouraging of a discriminatory climate
- Reinforcing of institutional sexism

Discussion Questions

1. How could you support a colleague who has been sexually harassed?

2. How could you help a client who has been sexually harassed?

3. What would be a plan for bringing back the information on sexual harassment to your field placement setting?

4. Is sexual harassment defined differently by different cultures?

5. What are three strategies that you could employ in your agency to help to eliminate sexual harassment?

Posters/Discussion Materials

University of Washington, School of Social Work

TELL SOMEONE

Reporting Incidents of Harassment Makes Sense!

Over one weekend, swastikas and other types of anti-Semitic graffiti were drawn on the School walls. After a group of students reported this to faculty and administration, the graffiti were removed, memos were sent to students, faculty, and staff regarding the incident, and a committee was established to explore ways to make the school a safer and more supportive environment for all people.

If you experience harassment in the School of Social Work or in a practicum agency, tell someone by calling Affirmative Action or the School of Social Work Ombudsman, or by talking with a faculty member.

Talking about harassment is one way to stop it and prevent its reoccurrence!

IS THIS HARASSMENT?

What would you do?

A professor in a research class assigns an article describing a study which was done on methods to change the sexual orientation of gays and lesbians. In the class discussion of this article, the ethical aspects of this kind of intervention were not discussed. Students leave the class feeling upset and angry.

Harassment is behavior that intimidates or demeans others. It can be verbal, written, or physical. If you experience harassment in the School of Social Work or in a practicum agency, tell someone by calling Affirmative Action or the School of Social Work Ombudsman, or by talking with a faculty member.

Talking about harassment is one way to stop it and prevent its reoccurrence!

IS THIS HARASSMENT?

What would you do?

> A lesbian student has been very active in student organizations and outspoken on gay and lesbian issues. One morning she arrives at the school and finds pornographic cartoons taped to her locker. She feels angry, frightened, and upset.

Harassment is behavior that intimidates or demeans others. It can be verbal, written, or physical. If you experience harassment in the School of Social Work or in a practicum agency, tell someone by calling Affirmative Action or the School of Social Work Ombudsman, or by talking with a faculty member.

Talking about harassment is one way to stop it and prevent its reoccurrence!

IS THIS HARASSMENT?

What would you do?

In a class discussion on family assessment, a student refers to one of her clients as a "chink." A number of students look uncomfortable but say nothing.

Harassment is behavior that intimidates or demeans others. It can be verbal, written, or physical. If you experience harassment in the School of Social Work or in a practicum agency, tell someone by calling Affirmative Action or the School of Social Work Ombudsman, or by talking with a faculty member.

Talking about harassment is one way to stop it and prevent its reoccurrence!

Peer Harassment: What Can Be Done?

What is peer harassment?

While most students at schools of social work behave in a friendly, collegial way, a small percentage of students engage in behavior that is harassing, intimidating, or demeaning to other students on the basis of their ethnic or cultural heritage, race, religion, age, marital status, physical disability or appearance, sexual orientation, gender, or identification with a particular group.

Verbal, written, or physical contact of a harassing or intimidating nature can be subtle or overt. Even subtle harassment can be extremely damaging to an individual. Example of peer harassment can include:

- violating another student's residence
- degrading jokes
- racial slurs
- defacing posters or flyers
- name calling
- hate mail or phone calls
- physical abuse
- unwanted touching or physical contact
- unwanted sexual advances
- pestering or street harassment
- demeaning graffiti

What effects can it have?

- interfere with your pursuit of an education
- undermine or lower your self-esteem
- cause you to fear for your personal safety
- affect your health
- limit your freedom of movement
- keep you from participating fully in the campus community
- make you distrustful of others

Why does it occur?

The reasons why people harass, degrade, or intimidate others are as varied as the kinds of incidents that occur. Incidents that appear to be, or are, intolerant, prejudiced, or bigoted can be the result of:

- miscommunication/ misunderstanding
- jealousy
- ignorance
- prejudice passed on by family and friends
- deliberate malice
- lack of exposure to those who are in some way different from oneself
- unresolved psychological issues
- accepting negative media stereotypes as true

What to do if you are the subject of peer harassment:

- Do not verbally or physically retaliate or respond to the harasser. Notify a campus official and report what happened.

- Keep a record of what happened, including when and where the incident(s) occurred. Try to get the name, phone number, and address of any witness.

- Tell someone: Report the incident to one of the offices listed in this brochure. If you prefer, you may bring along a friend or witness with you.

- If you believe you are in physical danger, contact the police.

Remember...

- Reporting is your right.

- No one deserves to be harassed or intimidated.

- This is your campus. Don't let anyone take away your right to participate freely in the campus community.

Six Things I've Always Wanted to Know About Harassment, But Was Afraid to Ask

Questions and Answers

Q: If I think I've been harassed, who can I go to?

A: You might choose anyone in the School community with whom you feel safe sharing this experience. As Ombudsmen, Vanessa Hodges in the School of Social Work and Lois Price Spratlen in HUB 301 are available.

Q: I think I was harassed, but I have no witnesses. Do I have a right to report it?

A: Yes, you always have a right to talk with the person of your choice about your experience. You deserve to be heard and supported.

Q: I felt harassed by another student in a class during fall quarter, and it's spring now. Can I still talk to someone?

A: Yes, you can talk with the person of your choice at any time. There is a statute of limitations only if you wish to make a formal complaint.

Myths and Facts

Myth: If I talk with anyone about the harassment I experienced, my professors will find out and make my school career miserable and/or prevent me from graduating.

Fact: Whoever you talk to about harassment is required to hold that information in confidence, and it will not be used against you in any way. Although professors (and staff) are legally required to report all incidents of sexual harassment to the Dean—who will inform the Human Rights Office, the Ombudsman for Sexual Harassment, or the Equal Employment Office—your confidentiality will be protected.

Myth: Harassment is defined as sexual touching or suggestions made by a male professor to a female student.

Fact: Harassment includes any inappropriate activity or remark based on gender, ethnicity, sexual orientation, physical ability, religious beliefs, or any other attribute. Harassment can occur between any two people, regardless of gender or status at the University.

Myth: People who experience harassment bring it on themselves by flaunting their differences.

Fact: No one deserves to be harassed for any reason. The University and the School of Social Work have policies of respecting diversity.